CTRL·ALT·DELETE

Matthew N. Lyons, It's Going Down,
K. Kersplebedeb, Bromma

KER
SPL
EBE
DEB
2017

Ctrl-Alt-Delete, edited by Kersplebedeb
ISBN: 978-1-894946-85-8

Kersplebedeb Publishing and Distribution
CP 63560
CCCP Van Horne
Montreal, Quebec
Canada H3W 3H8
email: info@kersplebedeb.com
web: www.kersplebedeb.com
         www.leftwingbooks.net

Copies available from AK Press: www.akpress.org

Printed in Canada

Contents

Preface

Kersplebedeb

This book addresses the origins and rise of the so-called "alt-right," the fascistic movement that grabbed headlines in the months leading up to the 2016 election of Donald Trump as president of the United States.

Understanding the alt-right is important for those who aim to resist the era in which we find ourselves. This is a movement that has the wind in its sails, embodying the resentments and frustrations of large swathes of America, intent on reasserting and reinforcing the supremacy of white men, to the detriment, exclusion, or even annihilation of everyone else. Even if the alt-right were to disappear tomorrow—sadly, something very unlikely—the political forces it currently contains would continue their march, just as historical dynamics in play would continue to provide them with recruits and avenues of advance.

Confronting this enemy—a task that can only be helped by *knowing* this enemy—is therefore high up on our "to do" list.

The first essay, Matthew Lyons's "Ctrl-Alt-Delete," is a thorough survey of the origins of the alt-right, a look at its constituent parts and beliefs at the present time, as well as observations about how its future relationship with the Trump administration may play out. Of particular interest, Lyons draws attention to the importance of sexism and misogyny within this movement, to its long-term "metapolitical" strategy, as well as to the tensions between the disparate groups that have found their home under its banner.

Lyons's essay was already in the works prior to the developments of 2016, part of a broader study of anti-systemic far right movements in the United States. That book, *Insurgent Supremacists: The U.S. Far Right's Challenge to State and Empire*, is due out from Kersplebedeb and PM Press in 2018. Given the rapid developments of the past few months, however, it was felt important to make his chapter on the alt-right available as soon as possible—therein lies the origin of this publication. It should also be noted that this essay will be made available online by Political Research Associates at www.altrightdelete.org for free download.

Supplementing "Ctrl-Alt-Delete" is an essay written by comrades from the *It's Going Down* website, "The Rich Kids of Fascism." This is a view from activists currently involved in opposing both the far right and the state, on the streets. As its title would imply, the essay's focus is on the elitist class politics of the alt-right, and how that sets it apart from other far right phenomena such as boneheads or militias. Surveying the alt-right's fortunes over the past few years, IGD show the role played by both the media, and white racist fears about the ongoing struggles of black people and immigrants in feeding this threat.

The two essays share much in perspective, but there are some notable differences in focus; each raises important questions of what to expect from the current far right surge, and more importantly, how to oppose it. Specifically, both texts underscore an important weakness of the alt-right, namely its lack of any effective street presence. It remains a conglomeration of elitists who meet at private symposia, and populist keyboard warriors who rarely leave their basements, all of whom seem to have experienced their lives before Trump as some kind of inner emigration from the hostile—supposedly anti-male and anti-white—world around them. While they have punched above their weight in the realm of public opinion, this lack of a street presence, if not remedied, will be a crucial factor in how things play out over the years to come. Our opponents are clearly aware of this, and already we can see their attempts to overcome this limitation, for instance in Andrew Anglin's proposed anti-Jewish march on Whitefish, Montana, or in "alt-lite" form in Gavin McInnes's Proud Boys Network.

A third text, "Black Genocide and the Alt-Right," unpacks much of what terms like "white nationalism" and "race realism" imply in the American context. Anti-black racism constitutes a baseline for far right politics, and the alt-right is no exception, despite the utopian pretentions of some of their more highbrow thinkers (when they're not dropping n-bombs and celebrating the murder of black youths, that is). This text is just a brief reminder of what these things mean.

Finally, "Notes on Trump," by Bromma, serves not so much as a counterpoint, as a contextualization. Not directly addressing the alt-right itself, Bromma's "Notes" posit that the election of Trump and the rise of the far right are not simple accidents of history, nor the result of some single failure on our side or success on theirs, but are conjoined expressions of a deep shift in the world economy. As he argues, "What's coming into view, semi-hidden underneath the frenzied soap opera of reactionary populism, is that the tide of globalization has crested and started to recede."

While it is important to not fall into the trap of viewing political and cultural phenomena ("superstructure") as being automatically set in stone by economic considerations ("structure"), we can nonetheless see that the latter often establish the possibilities of how the former may develop. Bromma's text therefore points to Trumpism, and the current prominence of the alt-right, as signs of a more intractable sea-change; even though they themselves may be defeated or neutralized, this deeper change signals that there will be more like them. Indeed, if we do not succeed in doing our job, it is likely that there will be a cascading series of lurches to the right, to authoritarianism, ultimately towards ramped up genocide and war.

This is not an optimistic view. While Trump and the alt-right benefited from an extraordinary confluence of factors—not least for each being the other—that there were deep structural factors at play would mean such a lurch was inevitable, if not now then soon enough. This is not "fascism," and the alt-right is different from the kind of mass reactionary movements the United States and Europe have seen in the past. But things are just getting started.

The alt-right is *one* expression of this reactionary moment. We must oppose them, but also prepare ourselves to oppose what might come next. Or what might hit us at the same time, from some other direction: after all, multiple xenophobic and far right forces are searching out opportunities in this new and treacherous zone, not just the ones discussed in this book.

Understanding our enemy can only help us turn the tide, or at least dam its flow. What's more, a thorough understanding of this opposing political force can also help us prepare for future far right iterations.

That is why this book is being offered now. A tool for work that needs doing. Let's get started.

K. Kersplebedeb
January 2017

Ctrl-Alt-Delete

An Antifascist Report
On the Alternative Right

Matthew N. Lyons

Maybe you first heard about them in the summer of 2015, when they promoted the insult "cuckservative" to attack Trump's opponents in the Republican primaries.[1] Maybe it was in August 2016, when Hillary Clinton denounced them as "a fringe element" that had "effectively taken over the Republican party."[2] Or maybe it was a couple of weeks after Trump's surprise defeat of Clinton, when a group of them were caught on camera giving the fascist salute in response to a speaker shouting "Hail Trump, hail our people, hail victory!"[3]

The alt-right helped Donald Trump get elected president, and Trump's campaign put the alt-right in the news. But the movement was active well before Trump announced his candidacy, and its relationship with Trump has been more complex and more qualified than many critics realize. The alt-right is just

---

1. David Weigel. "'Cuckservative'—the conservative insult of the month, explained." *The Washington Post* (online), July 29, 2015.
2. Abby Ohlheiser and Caitlin Dewey. "Hillary Clinton's alt-right speech, annotated." *The Washington Post* (online), August 25, 2016.
3. Daniel Lombroso and Yoni Appelbaum. "'Hail Trump!': White Nationalists Salute the President Elect." *The Atlantic* (online), November 21, 2016.

one of multiple dangerous forces associated with Trump, but it's the one that has attracted the greatest notoriety. However, it's not accurate to argue, as many critics have, that "alt-right" is just a deceptive code-phrase meant to hide the movement's white supremacist or neonazi politics. This is a movement with its own story, and for those concerned about the seemingly sudden resurgence of far right politics in the United States, it is a story worth exploring.

The alt-right, short for "Alternative Right," is a loosely organized far right movement that shares a contempt for both liberal multiculturalism and mainstream conservatism; a belief that some people are inherently superior to others; a strong internet presence and embrace of specific elements of online culture; and a self-presentation as being new, hip, and irreverent.[4] Based primarily in the United States, alt-right ideology combines white nationalism, misogyny, antisemitism, and authoritarianism in various forms and in political styles ranging from intellectual argument to violent invective. White nationalism constitutes the movement's center of gravity, but some alt-rightists are more focused on reasserting male dominance or other forms of elitism rather than race. The alt-right has little in the way of formal organization, but has used internet memes effectively to gain visibility, rally supporters, and target opponents. Most alt-rightists have rallied behind Trump's presidential bid, yet as a rule alt-rightists regard the existing political system as hopeless and call for replacing the United States with one or more racially defined homelands.

This report offers an overview of the alt-right's history, beliefs, and relationship with other political forces. Part I traces the movement's ideological origins in paleoconservatism and

---

4. I use the term "far right" to refer to political forces that (a) promote human inequality based on race, gender, or other factors as natural or inevitable and (b) reject the legitimacy of the US political system. This definition is specific to the United States today and does not necessarily apply to other times or places.

the European New Right, and its development since Richard Spencer launched the original *AlternativeRight.com* website in 2010. Part 2 surveys the major political currents that comprise or overlap with the alt-right, which include in their ranks white nationalists, members of the antifeminist "manosphere," male tribalists, right-wing anarchists, and neoreactionaries. Part 3 focuses on the alt-right's relationship with the Trump presidential campaign, including movement debates about political strategy, online political tactics, and its relationship to a network of conservative supporters and popularizers known as the "alt-lite." A concluding section offers preliminary thoughts on the alt-right's prospects and the potential challenges it will face under the incoming Trump administration.

PART I
ORIGINS AND DEVELOPMENT

IDEOLOGICAL ROOTS

Two intellectual currents played key roles in shaping the early Alternative Right: paleoconservatism and the European New Right.

Paleoconservatives can trace their lineage back to the "Old Right" of the 1930s, which opposed New Deal liberalism, and to the America First movement of the early 1940s, which opposed US entry into World War II. To varying degrees, many of the America Firsters were sympathetic to fascism and fascist claims of a sinister Jewish-British conspiracy. In the early 1950s, this current supported Senator Joe McCarthy's witch-hunting crusade, which extended red-baiting to target representatives of the centrist Eastern Establishment. After McCarthy, the America First/anti-New Deal Right was largely submerged in a broader "fusionist" conservative movement, in which Cold War anticommunism served as the glue holding different rightist currents together. But when the Soviet bloc collapsed between 1989 and 1991, this anticommunist alliance unraveled, and old debates reemerged.[5]

In the 1980s, devotees of the Old Right began calling themselves paleoconservatives as a reaction against neoconservatives, those often formerly liberal and leftist intellectuals who were then gaining influential positions in right-wing think-tanks and the Reagan administration. The first neocons were predominantly Jewish and Catholic, which put them outside the ranks of old guard conservatism. Neocons promoted an aggressive foreign policy to spread US "democracy" throughout the world and supported a close alliance with Israel, but they also favored nonrestrictive immigration policies and, to a limited extent, social welfare programs. Paleoconservatives regarded the neocons as usurpers and closet leftists, and in the post-Soviet era they criticized military interventionism, free trade, immigration, globalization, and the welfare state. They also spoke out against Washington's close alliance with Israel, often in terms that had anti-Jewish undertones. Paleoconservatives tended to be unapologetic champions of European Christian culture, and some of them gravitated toward white nationalism, advocating a society in which white people, their values, interests, and concerns would always be explicitly preeminent. To some extent they began to converge with more hardline white supremacists during this period.[6]

These positions attracted little elite support, and after Reagan paleocons were mostly frozen out of political power. But they attracted significant popular support. In 1992 and 1996, Patrick Buchanan won millions of votes in Republican

---

5. Chip Berlet and Matthew N. Lyons. *Right-Wing Populism in America: Too Close for Comfort.* (New York: Guilford Press, 2000), 145–47, 160–61.
6. Ibid., 243–44, 283–84.

presidential primaries by emphasizing paleocon themes. Paleocons also played key roles in building the anti-immigrant and neo-Confederate movements in the '90s, and influenced the Patriot movement, which exploded briefly in the mid-90s around fears that globalist elites were plotting to impose a tyrannical world government on the United States. Some self-described libertarians, such as former Congressmember Ron Paul, embraced paleoconservative positions on culture and foreign policy.[7] After the September 11th attacks in 2001, the resurgence of military interventionism and neoconservatives' prominent roles in the George W. Bush administration solidified the paleocons' position as political outsiders.[8]

The alt-right's other significant forerunner, the European New Right (ENR), developed along different lines. The ENR began in France in the late 1960s and then spread to other European countries, as an initiative among far right intellectuals to rework fascist ideology, largely by appropriating elements from other political traditions—including the Left—to mask their fundamental rejection of the principle of human equality.[9] European New Rightists championed "biocultural diversity" against the homogenization supposedly brought by liberalism and globalization. They argued that true antiracism requires separating racial and ethnic groups to protect their unique cultures, and that true feminism defends natural gender differences, instead of supposedly forcing women to "divest

---

7. Rachel Tabachnick and Frank L. Cocozzelli. "Nullification, Neo-Confederates, and the Revenge of the Old Right." *Political Research Associates* (online), Nov. 22, 2013.

8. Matthew N. Lyons, "Fragmented Nationalism: Right-Wing Responses to September 11 in Historical Context." *The Pennsylvania Magazine of History and Biography* 127, no 4 (October, 2003), 398–404.

9. Roger Griffin, "Plus ça change! The Fascist Legacy in the Metapolitics of the Nouvelle Droite." Chapter for *The Development of the Radical Right in France 1890–1995*. (London: Routledge, 2000). Anton Shekhovtsov, "Aleksandr Dugin's Neo-Eurasianism: The New Right à la Russe." *Religion Compass* 3, no. 4 (2009): 697–716.

themselves of their femininity." ENR writers also rejected the principle of universal human rights as "a strategic weapon of Western ethnocentrism" that stifles cultural diversity.[10]

European New Rightists dissociated themselves from traditional fascism in various other ways as well. In the wake of France's defeat by anticolonial forces in Algeria, they advocated anti-imperialism rather than expansionism and a federated "empire" of regionally based, ethnically homogeneous communities, rather than a big, centralized state. Instead of organizing a mass movement to seize state power, they advocated a "metapolitical" strategy that would gradually transform the political and intellectual culture as a precursor to transforming institutions and systems. In place of classical fascism's familiar leaders and ideologues, European New Rightists championed more obscure far rightist intellectuals of the 1920s, '30s, and beyond, such as Julius Evola of Italy, Ernst Jünger and Carl Schmitt of Germany, and Corneliu Codreanu of Romania.

ENR ideology began to get attention in the United States in the 1990s,[11] resonating with paleoconservatism on various themes, notably opposition to multicultural societies, nonwhite immigration, and globalization. On other issues, the two movements tended to be at odds: reflecting their roots in classical fascism but in sharp contrast to paleocons, European New Rightists were hostile to liberal individualism and laissez faire capitalism, and many of them rejected Christianity in favor of paganism. Nonetheless, some kind of dialog between paleocon and ENR ideas held promise for Americans seeking to develop a white nationalist movement outside of traditional neonazi/Ku Klux Klan circles.

---

10. Alain de Benoist and Charles Champetier, "Manifesto of the French New Right in the Year 2000." (online)

11. In the 1990s, the ex-leftist journal *Telos* was instrumental in translating European New Right texts into English and engaging with ENR ideas. See for example the *Telos* Winter 1993–Fall 1994 (nos. 98-99) special double issue on "The French New Right: New Right-New Left-New Paradigm?"

EARLY YEARS AND GROWTH

The term "alternative right" was introduced by Richard Spencer in 2008, when he was managing editor at the paleocon and libertarian *Taki's Magazine*. At *Taki's Magazine* the phrase was used as a catch-all for a variety of right-wing voices at odds with the conservative establishment, including paleocons, libertarians, and white nationalists.[12] Two years later Spencer left to found a new publication, *AlternativeRight.com*, as "an online magazine of radical traditionalism." Joining Spencer were two senior contributing editors, Peter Brimelow (whose anti-immigrant VDARE Foundation sponsored the project) and Paul Gottfried (one of paleoconservatism's founders and one of its few Jews). *AlternativeRight.com* quickly became a popular forum among dissident rightist intellectuals, especially younger ones. The magazine published works of old-school "scientific" racism along with articles from or about the European New Right, Italian far right philosopher Julius Evola, and figures from Germany's interwar Conservative Revolutionary movement. There were essays by National-Anarchist Andrew Yeoman, libertarian and Pat Buchanan supporter Justin Raimondo of *Antiwar.com*, male tribalist Jack Donovan, and black conservative Elizabeth Wright.[13]

AlternativeRight.com developed ties with a number of other white nationalist intellectual publications, which eventually became associated with the term Alternative Right. Some of its main partners included VDARE.*com*; Jared Taylor's *American Renaissance*, whose conferences attracted both antisemites and right-wing Jews; *The Occidental Quarterly* and its online magazine, *The Occidental Observer*, currently edited by prominent

---

12. See, for example, Richard Spencer, "The Conservative Write." *Taki's Magazine*, Aug. 6, 2008; Kevin DeAnna, "The Alternative Right." *Taki's Magazine*, July 26, 2009; and Jack Hunter, "Whither the Alternative Right?" *Taki's Magazine*, Nov. 3, 2009.

13. Matthew N. Lyons, "AlternativeRight.com: Paleoconservatism for the 21st Century." *Three Way Fight* (online). September 19, 2010.

antisemitic intellectual Kevin MacDonald; and Counter-Currents Publishing, which was founded in 2010 to "create an intellectual movement in North America that is analogous to the European New Right" and "lay the intellectual groundwork for a white ethnostate in North America."[14]

In 2011, Richard Spencer became head of the white nationalist think-tank National Policy Institute (NPI) and its affiliated Washington Summit Publishers. He turned *AlternativeRight.com* over to other editors the following year, then shut it down completely, establishing a new online magazine, *Radix*, in its place. (The other editors then reestablished *Alternative Right* as a blog.) Compared with *AlternativeRight.com*'s broad ideological approach, Spencer's later entities were more sharply focused on promoting white nationalism. Starting in 2011, NPI held a series of high-profile conferences that brought together intellectuals and activists from various branches of the movement. In 2014, the think-tank, together with supporters of Russian ENR theorist Aleksandr Dugin, cosponsored a "pan-European" conference in Budapest, although the Hungarian government deported Spencer and denied Dugin a visa.[15]

Starting in 2015, a much wider array of writers and online activists embraced the alt-right moniker. As *Anti-Fascist News* put it, "the 'alt right' now often means an internet focused string of commentators, blogs, Twitter accounts, podcasters, and *Reddit* trolls, all of which combine scientific racism, romantic nationalism, and deconstructionist neo-fascist ideas to create a white nationalist movement that has almost no backwards connection with neonazis and the KKK."[16] Some online centers

---

14. Greg Johnson, "Theory & Practice." *Counter-Currents Publishing* (online), September 2010.

15. James Kirchick, "American Racist Richard Spencer Gets to Play the Martyr in Hungary." *The Daily Beast* (online), October 7, 2014.

16. Antifascist Front, "Alternative Internet Racism: Alt Right and the New Fascist Branding." *Anti-Fascist News* (online), December 18, 2015.

of this larger, more amorphous alt-right included the image-board websites *4chan* and *8chan*, various *Reddit* sub-communities, and *The Right Stuff* blog and podcasts. Some alt-right outfits offered neonazi-oriented politics (such as *The Daily Stormer* and the Traditionalist Youth Network), while others did not (such as *Occidental Dissent*, *The Unz Review*, *Vox Popoli*, and *Chateau Heartiste*).

On many sites, alt-right politics were presented in terms intended to be as inflammatory as possible, bucking a decades-old trend among US far rightists to tone down their beliefs for mass consumption. Previously, antisemitic propagandist Willis Carto and former Ku Klux Klan leader David Duke had made careers of dressing up fascism as "populism" or "conservatism"; now alt-rightists confidently derided antifascism in the way 1960s radicals had derided anticommunism: "We might not all be proper fascists," *The Right Stuff* columnist Lawrence Murray wrote in 2015, "but we're all a little fash whether we want to be or not. We're fashy goys—we think a lot of nasty thoughts that keep leftists up at night during their struggle sessions. Might as well embrace it …"[17]

The alt-right's rapid growth partly reflected trends in internet culture, where anonymity and the lack of face-to-face contact have fostered widespread use of insults, bullying, and supremacist speech. More immediately, it reflected recent political developments, such as a backlash against the Black Lives Matter movement and, above all, Donald Trump's presidential candidacy. A majority of alt-rightists supported Trump's campaign because of his anti-immigrant proposals; defamatory rhetoric against Mexicans, Muslims, women, and others; and his clashes with mainstream conservatives and the Republican Party establishment.

17. Lawrence Murray, "Fashism." *The Right Stuff* (online), October 24, 2015.

Part 2
Major Ideological Currents

WHITE NATIONALISTS, HIGH- AND LOW-BROW

The original *AlternativeRight.com* magazine helped set the parameters of alt-right white nationalism. In "Why an Alternative Right is Necessary," published in 2010 soon after the magazine was launched, columnist Richard Hoste offered a paleocon-style criticism of the War on Terror and mainstream conservatives, coupled with a blunt new emphasis on race:

> "One would think that the odds of a major terrorist attack happening would depend on how many Muslims are allowed to live in the United States. Reducing Islamic immigration in the name of fighting terror would receive widespread public support, be completely practical in a way installing a puppet regime in Afghanistan wouldn't, and not lead us to kill or torture anybody.... The idea that nothing must be done to stop the March Of Diversity is so entrenched in the minds of those considered of the Right that they will defend America policing the entire planet, torture, indefinite detentions, and a nation on permanent war footing but won't mention immigration restriction or racial profiling.

> "We've known for a while through neuroscience and cross-adoption studies—if common sense wasn't enough—that individuals differ in their inherent capabilities. The races do, too, with whites and Asians on the top and blacks at the bottom. The Alternative Right takes it for granted that equality of opportunity means inequality of results for various classes, races, and the two sexes. Without ignoring the importance of culture, we see

> Western civilization as a unique product of the European gene pool."[18]

A few months later, Greg Johnson at *Counter-Currents Publishing* declared that

> "The survival of whites in North America and around the world is threatened by a host of bad ideas and policies: egalitarianism, the denial of biological race and sex differences, feminism, emasculation, racial altruism, ethnomasochism and xenophilia, multiculturalism, liberalism, capitalism, non-white immigration, individualism, consumerism, materialism, hedonism, anti-natalism, etc."

He also warned that white people would not survive unless they "work to reduce Jewish power and influence" and "regain political control over a viable national homeland or homelands."[19]

In 2016, following the Alternative Right's rapid growth, Lawrence Murray in *The Right Stuff* proposed a summary of the movement's "big tent" philosophy: inequality of both individuals and populations is "a fact of life"; "races and their national subdivisions exist and compete for resources, land and influence"; white people are being suppressed and "must be allowed to take their own side"; men and women have separate roles and heterosexual monogamy is crucial for racial survival; "the franchise should be limited" because universal democracy "gives power to the worst and shackles the fittest"; and "Jewish elites are opposed to our entire program."[20] Alfred W. Clark in *Radix* offered a slightly different summary. In his view, alt-rightists recognize human biodiversity; reject universalism; want to

---

18. Richard Hoste, "Why an Alternative Right is Necessary." *AlternativeRight.com*, February 24, 2010.

19. Johnson op cit., 2010 (online).

20. Lawrence Murray, "The Fight for the Alt-Right: The Rising Tide of Ideological Autism Against Big-Tent Supremacy." *The Right Stuff* (online), March 6, 2016.

reverse Third World immigration into the West; are skeptical of free trade and free market ideology; oppose mainstream Christianity from a variety of religious viewpoints (traditionalist Christian, neo-pagan, atheist, and agnostic); and often (but not always) support Donald Trump. Unlike Murray, Clark noted that alt-rightists disagree about the "Jewish question," but generally agree "that Jews have disproportionately been involved in starting left-wing movements of the last 150 years."[21]

Alt-rightists have promoted these ideas in different ways. Some have used moderate-sounding intellectual tones, often borrowed from the European New Right's euphemistic language about respecting "difference" and protecting "biocultural diversity." For example, the National Policy Institute has promoted "Identitarianism," a concept that was developed by the French New Right and popularized by the French group *Bloc Identitaire*. In 2015, Richard Spencer introduced an NPI essay contest for young writers on the theme, "Why I'm An Identitarian":

> "Identitarianism ... eschews nationalist chauvinism, as well as the meaningless, petty nationalism that is tolerated, even encouraged, by the current world system. That said, Identitarianism is itself not a universal value system, like Leftism, monotheism, and most contemporary versions of 'conservatism.' To the contrary, Identitarianism is fundamentally about **difference**, about culture as an expression of a certain people at a certain time .... Identitarianism acknowledges the **incommensurable** nature of different peoples and cultures—and thus looks forward to a world of true diversity and multiculturalism."[22]

---

21. Alfred W. Clark, "What is the #Altright?" *Radix* (online), January 20, 2016.

22. Richard B. Spencer, "Identitarianism—A Conversation Starter." *Radix* (online), June 15, 2015.

Very different versions of alt-right politics are available elsewhere. *The Right Stuff* website uses a mocking, ironic tone, with rotating tag lines such as "Your rational world is a circle jerk"; "Non-aggression is the triumph of weakness"; "Democracy is an interracial porno"; "Obedience to lawful authority is the foundation of manly character"; and "Life isn't fair. Sucks for you, but I don't care." An article by "Darth Stirner," titled "Fascist Libertarianism: For a Better World," further illustrated this style:

> "*Dear libertarian, take the rose colored glasses of racial egalitarianism off. Look around and see that other races don't even disguise their hatred of you. Even though you don't think in terms of race, rest assured that they do. Humanity is composed of a series of racial corporations. They stick together, and if we don't … Western civilization is doomed. […]*

> "*Progressives, communists, and degenerates of various stripes will need to be interned—at least during the transition period. Terrorism and guerrilla warfare can be prevented with this measure. In the instance of a coup d'état it would be reasonable to detain every person who might conceivably be an enemy of the right-wing revolution. Rather than starving or torturing them they should be treated well with the highest standard of living reasonably possible. Most of them will simply be held until the war is over and the winner is clear. This is actually much more humane than allowing a hotly contested civil war to occur.*"[23]

---

23. Darth Stirner, "Fascist Libertarianism: For a Better World." *The Right Stuff* (online), January 23, 2013.

The *Right Stuff* doesn't just offer quasi-irony, however, but also naked bigotry, as summarized by *Anti-Fascist News*:

> "[On *The Right Stuff*] they choose to openly use racial slurs, degrade women and rape survivors, mock the holocaust and call for violence against Jews. Their podcast, The Daily Shoah, which is a play on The Daily Show and the Yiddish term for The Holocaust, is a roundtable discussion of different racists broadcasting under pseudonyms. Here they do voice 'impressions' of Jews, and consistently use terms like 'Nig Nog,' 'Muds['] (referring to 'mud races,' meaning non-white), and calling people of African descent 'Dingos.' The N-word, homophobic slurs, and calls for enforced cultural patriarchy and heteronormativity are commonplace....
> The use of rhetoric like this is almost entirely missing from groups like American Renaissance, Counter-Currents, Radix Journal, Alternative Right, and even Stormfront, the main hub for racist groups who recently banned swastikas and racial slurs."[24]

Anti-Fascist News argues that different branches of the Alternative Right use different language to appeal to different target audiences. "The Right Stuff tries to mimic the aggression and reactionary insults of right-wing talk radio like Rush Limbaugh, while Radix would love to look a lot more like that trendy Critical Theory journal young grad students are clamoring to be published in."[25] This is more division of labor than factional conflict, as a number of alt-right intellectual figures have appeared on *The Right Stuff* podcasts, for example.

Stylistic differences aside, though, alt-rightists have also disagreed about substantive issues. One of the biggest points

---

24. Antifascist Front. "#Cuckservative: How the 'Alt Right' Took Off Their Masks and Revealed Their White Hoods." *Anti-Fascist News* (online), August 16, 2015.
25. Ibid.

of contention has been whether white nationalists should work with Jews, or at least some Jews. Anti-Jewish bigotry and scapegoating have been prevalent across most of the movement, but with important variations and exceptions. For the minority of alt-rightists who identify with neonazism, such as Andrew Anglin of *The Daily Stormer*, uncompromising antisemitism is the overriding core principle.[26] And for many others, Jews are a major existential threat. To *The Right Stuff* blogger "Auschwitz Soccer Ref," Jews as a group have engaged in "2,000 years of non-stop treachery and backstabbing" and are "remorseless enemies who seek the destruction of the people they hate, which is us." As a result, "anyone who self-identifies as a Jew or anyone who makes excuses for a continued Jewish presence in White homelands should be unapologetically excluded from this movement, and none of these people should ever be allowed to speak at alt right conferences no matter how pro-White they may seem."[27]

Not all alt-rightists agree. *American Renaissance*, one of the movement's central institutions, pioneered a version of white nationalism that avoided antisemitism. Besides publishing Jewish authors, both Jews and antisemites have been welcome at AmRen events as long as they set aside their disagreements.[28] Richard Spencer, too, repeatedly welcomed Jewish writers and cited them as useful contributors to the movement.

Even alt-rightists who view Jews as dangerous outsiders don't necessarily regard them as the embodiment of pure evil. Serbian-American author Srdja Trifkovic wrote that "the Jews" had disproportionately contributed to the erosion of European civilization. Nevertheless, he hoped for an alliance with Jews

26. Andrew Anglin, "Intensified Jewing: Vox Covers the Alt-Right." *The Daily Stormer* (online), April 18, 2016.
27. Auschwitz Soccer Ref, "Zero Tolerance: Why Aren't White Nationalists and Jewish Nationalists Fellow Travelers?" *The Right Stuff* (online), April 11, 2016.
28. Jared Taylor, "Jews and American Renaissance." *American Renaissance* (online), April 14, 2006.

against their common enemy, "the brown, black, and yellow multitudes" whose eventual attacks on the Jewish community might "easily exceed in ferocity and magnitude the events of 1942–45."[29] Similarly, *Counter-Currents* writer M.K. Lane described Jews as "a self-segregating and culturally arrogant people, a people who refuse to assimilate [and] who even when they do ostensibly assimilate, cause even greater harm than they did before desegregating." Yet Lane also hopes that a significant number of Jews could be won over to ally with white nationalism since, "if we go down, they go down." Of course, in such an alliance white nationalists "must not allow ourselves to become stooges." Jews "living in our midst … could either be allowed to live in their own communities, assimilate in small numbers, or move to Israel. Anything as long as they refrain from subverting our societies …"[30]

MANOSPHERE

While white nationalism has been central to the Alternative Right, patriarchal politics have played an increasingly important—and increasingly poisonous—role in the movement. The original *AlternativeRight.com* featured a range of views on gender, from patriarchal traditionalism to a kind of quasi-feminism. A number of male contributors expressed concern that their branch of the Right had attracted few women. Publisher and novelist Alex Kurtagic argued in 2011 that women and men had distinct natural roles, but that the white nationalist movement needed both:

29. Eugene Girin, "Is the Alt Right Anti-Semitic?" *AlternativeRight.com*, July 29, 2010. [Reposted in *Radix* (online).]
30. M. K. Lane, "Will Jews Change Sides?" *Counter-Currents Publishing* (online), February 17, 2016.

> "Women are far more than nurturers: they are especially
> proficient at networking, community building, consensus
> building, multi-tasking, and moral and logistical sup-
> port provision. These are all essential in any movement
> involving community outreach and where user-friendly,
> low-key, non-threatening forms of recruitment are advis-
> able.... Women can create a much broader comfort
> zone around hardcore political activism through organis-
> ing a wide range of community, human, and support-
> oriented activities..."[31]

Andrew Yeoman of Bay Area National Anarchists argued
more pointedly that sexist behavior by male alt-rightists was
driving women away:

> "Many women won't associate with our ideas. Why is
> this important? Because it leaves half our people out
> of the struggle. The women that do stick around have
> to deal with a constant litany of abuse and frequent
> courtship invitations from unwanted suitors.... nothing
> says 'you're not important to us' [more] than sexualizing
> women in the movement. Don't tell me that's not an
> issue. I've seen it happen in all kinds of radical circles,
> and ours is the worst for it."[32]

As the Alternative Right has grown, it has abandoned this
kind of self-criticism and debate about gender politics. Going
beyond traditionalist claims about the sanctity of the family and natural gender roles, alt-rightists have embraced an
intensely misogynistic ideology, portraying women as irrational, vindictive creatures who need and want men to rule

---

31. Alex Kurtagic, "Women as a Measure of Credibility." *AlternativeRight.com*
(online), May 25, 2011.
32. Quoted in Lyons op cit. 2010.

over them and who should be stripped of any political role.[33] The Traditionalist Youth Network claims that "women's biological drives are contrary to the best interests of civilization and...the past century or so of women's enfranchisement and liberation has been detrimental to societal stability." But the group frames this position as relatively moderate because, unlike some rightists, they don't believe "that women are central to the destruction of Western Civilization"—they are simply being manipulated by the Jews.[34] *The Daily Stormer* has banned female contributors and called for limiting women's roles in the movement, sparking criticism from women on the more old school white nationalist discussion site *Stormfront*. Far right blogger Matt Forney asserts that "Trying to 'appeal' to women is an exercise in pointlessness.... it's not that women should be unwelcome [in the alt-right], it's that they're unimportant."[35]

A big reason for this shift toward hardline woman-hating is that the alt-right has become closely intertwined with the so-called manophere, an online antifeminist male subculture that has grown rapidly in recent years, largely outside traditional right-wing networks. The manosphere includes various overlapping circles, such as Men's Rights Activists (MRAs), who argue that the legal system and media unfairly discriminate against men; Pickup Artists (PUAs), who help men learn how to manipulate women into having sex with them; Men Going Their Own Way (MGTOWs), who protest women's supposed dominance by avoiding relationships with them; and others.[36]

---

33. Matthew N. Lyons, "Alt-right: more misogynistic than many neonazis." *Three Way Fight* (online), December 3, 2016.

34. Traditionalist Youth Network, "Jews Destroy Women: A Response to 'Women Destroy Nations.'" *Traditionalist Youth Network* (online), February 2016.

35. Danielle Paquette, "The alt-right isn't only about white supremacy. It's about white male supremacy." *Chicago Tribune* (online), November 25, 2016.

36. Jeff Sharlet, "Are You Man Enough for the Men's Rights Movement?" *GQ* (online), February 3, 2014.

Manospherians have emphasized male victimhood—the false belief that men in US society are oppressed or disempowered by feminism or by women in general. This echoes the concept of "reverse racism," the idea that white Americans face unfair discrimination, which white nationalists have promoted since the 1970s.

Some manospherians are family-centered traditionalists while others celebrate a more predatory sexuality. Daryush Valizadeh, who writes at the PUA site *Return of Kings* under the name Roosh V, embodies this tension. He argues that the nuclear family with one father and one mother is the healthiest unit for raising children, and socialism is damaging because it makes women dependent on the government and discourages them from using their "feminine gifts" to "land a husband." Yet Valizadeh has also written ten how-to books for male sex tourists with titles such as *Bang Ukraine* and *Bang Iceland*. Valizadeh doesn't dwell on his own glaring inconsistency, but does suggest in his article, "What is Neomasculinity?," that the dismantling of patriarchal rules has forced men to pursue "game" as a defensive strategy "to hopefully land some semblance of a normal relationship."[37]

Like the alt-right, manosphere discourse ranges from intellectual arguments to raw invective, although the line between them is often blurred. Paul Elam's *A Voice for Men*, founded in 2009, became one of the manosphere's most influential websites with intentionally provocative articles arguing, for example, that the legal system was so heavily stacked against men that rape trial jurors should vote to acquit "even in the face of overwhelming evidence that the charges are true."[38] Elam also "satirically" declared October "Bash a Violent Bitch Month,"

---

37. Roosh V [Daryush Valizadeh], "What is Neomasculinity?" *Roosh V* (online), May 6, 2015.
38. Paul Elam, "Jury duty at a rape trial? Acquit!" *A Voice for Men* (online), July 20, 2010.

urging men to fight back against physically abusive female partners. He offered "satire" such as:

> "I don't mean subdue them, or deliver an open handed
> pop on the face to get them to settle down. I mean
> literally to grab them by the hair and smack their face
> against the wall till the smugness of beating on someone
> because you know they won't fight back drains from their
> nose with a few million red corpuscles."[39]

Manospherians also tend to promote homophobia and trans-phobia, which is consistent with their efforts to re-impose rigid gender roles and identities. At *Return of Kings*, Valizadeh has denounced the legalization of same-sex marriage as "one phase of a degenerate march to persecute heterosexuals, both legally and socially, while acclimating young children to the homo-sexual lifestyle."[40] On the same website, Matt Forney warned that trans women who have sex with cis men might be guilty of "rape by fraud."[41] At the same time, some manosphere sites have sought to reach out to gay men. *A Voice for Men* published a series of articles by Matthew Lye that were later collected into the e-book *The New Gay Liberation: Escaping the Fag End of Feminism*, which Paul Elam described as "a scorching indict-ment of feminist hatred of all things male."[42]

One of the events that brought the manosphere to public attention was the Gamergate controversy. Starting in 2014, a

---

39. Paul Elam, "October is the fifth annual Bash a Violent Bitch Month," *A Voice for Men* (online), September 30, 2015.

40. Roosh V [Daryush Valizadeh], "Why Homosexual Marriage Matters For Straight Men." *Return of Kings*, October 12, 2015 (cached online at https://archive.is/HzSIx#selection-139.0–139.16).

41. Matt Forney, "Are Transsexuals Who Sleep With Straight Men Guilty of Rape?" *Return of Kings* (online), December 8, 2014.

42. Paul Elam, "Andy Bob exposes feminist hatred of gay men in new book." *A Voice for Men* (online), January 7, 2016.

number of women who worked in—or were critical of sexism in—the video game industry were subjected to large-scale campaigns of harassment, coordinated partly with the #Gamergate Twitter hashtag. Supporters of Gamergate claimed that that campaign was a defense of free speech and journalistic ethics and against political correctness, but it included streams of misogynistic abuse, rape and death threats, as well as doxxing (public releases of personal information), which caused several women to leave their homes out of fear for their physical safety.[43] The Gamergate campaign took the pervasive, systematic pattern of threats and abuse that has been long used to silence women on the internet, and sharpened it into a focused weapon of attack.[44] Gamergate, in turn, strongly influenced the alt-right's own online activism, as I discuss below.

There is significant overlap between the manosphere and the alt-right. Both are heavily active on discussion websites such as *4chan*, *8chan*, and *Reddit*, and a number of prominent alt-rightists—such as Forney, Theodore Beale (pseudonym: "Vox Day"), James Weidmann ("Roissy"), and Andrew Auernheimer ("weev")—have also been active in the manosphere. Many other alt-rightists have absorbed and promoted manosphere versions of gender ideology.

But there have also been tensions between the two rightist movements. In 2015, Valizadeh ("Roosh V") began to build a connection with the Alternative Right, attending an NPI conference and quoting extensively from antisemite Kevin MacDonald in a lengthy post about "The Damaging Effects of Jewish Intellectualism And Activism On Western Culture."[45]

---

43. Stephen Totilo, "Another Woman in Gaming Flees Home Following Death Threats." *Kotaku* (online), October 11, 2014.

44. Amanda Hess, "Why Women Aren't Welcome on the Internet." *Pacific Standard* (online), January 6, 2014.

45. Roosh V [Daryush Valizadeh], "The Damaging Effects of Jewish Intellectualism And Activism On Western Culture." *Return of Kings* (online), May 4, 2015.

Some alt-rightists responded favorably. One blogger commented that the manosphere was "not as stigmatized" as white nationalism and the alt-right, and suggested hopefully that, "since the Manosphere has a very broad appeal it is possible that bloggers such as Roosh and Dalrock [a Christian manospherian] might serve as a stepping stone to guide formerly apathetic men towards the Alternative Right."[46] Matt Parrott of the Traditionalist Youth Network praised Valizadeh's "What is Neomasculinity?" as "a masterful synthesis of human biodiversity knowledge, radical traditionalist principle, and pragmatic modern dating experience."[47]

But the relationship soured quickly, largely because Valizadeh is Persian American. Although Andrew Anglin of *The Daily Stormer* tweeted that Valizadeh was "a civilized and honorable man,"[48] many white nationalists denounced him as non-white and an enemy. One tweeted that he was "a greasy Iranian" who "goes to Europe to defile white women and write books about it."[49] After studying Valizadeh's accounts of his own sex tourism, *Counter-Currents Publishing* editor-in-chief Greg Johnson concluded that Roosh "is either a rapist or a fraud" and "it is not just feminist hysteria to describe Roosh as a rape advocate." More broadly, Johnson wrote, "for all its benefits … the manosphere morally corrupts men. It does not promote the resurgence of traditional and biologically based sexual norms."[50] Valizadeh responded by blogging "The Alt

---

46. Dota, "Manosphere Rising." *Alternative Right* (online), May 14, 2015.

47. Matt Parrott, "An Endorsement of Roosh's 'Neomasculinity' Manifesto." *Traditionalist Youth Network* (online), May 2015 [updated 19 January 2016].

48. David Futrelle, "Hitler-loving dudes named Andrew agree: Roosh V is a-OK! (Even though he's not white.)" *We Hunted the Mammoth* (online), August 15, 2015.

49. David Futrelle, "Roosh V shocked to discover that white supremacist movement is full of white supremacists." *We Hunted the Mammoth* (online), February 24, 2016.

50. Greg Johnson, "Roosh Really is a Rape Advocate (& a Rapist, if He's Telling the Truth)." *Counter-Currents Publishing* n.d. (archived online at https://archive.is/T66uL)

Right Is Worse Than Feminism in Attempting to Control Male Sexual Behavior."[51]

MALE TRIBALISM

Jack Donovan, an early contributor to *AlternativeRight.com* who has stayed active in the alt-right as it has grown, offers a related but distinct version of male supremacist ideology. In a series of books and articles over the past decade, Donovan has advocated a system of patriarchy based on "tribal" comradeship among male warriors. Drawing on evolutionary psychology, he argues that in the past men have mostly organized themselves into small, close-knit "gangs," which fostered true masculinity and men's natural dominance over women. Yet modern "globalist civilization" "requires the abandonment of human scale identity groups for 'one world tribe.'" A combination of "feminists, elite bureaucrats, and wealthy men," he writes, has promoted male passivity and put women in a dominant role.[52]

Unlike Christian rightists, who argue that feminism misleads women into betraying their true interests, Donovan sees feminism as an expression of women's basic nature, which is "to calm men down and enlist their help at home, raising children, and fixing up the grass hut." Today, he argues, feminists' supposed alliance with globalist elites reflects this: "Women are better suited to and better served by the globalism and consumerism of modern democracies that promote security, no-strings attached sex and shopping."[53]

---

51. Roosh V [Daryush Valizadeh], "The Alt Right Is Worse Than Feminism in Attempting to Control Male Sexual Behavior." *Return of Kings* (online), February 22, 2016; Futrelle 2016 op cit.

52. Jack Donovan, *The Way of Men*. (Milwaukie, Ore.: Dissonant Hum.: 2012), 138–9.

53. Ibid., 137, 148.

Donovan's social and political ideal is a latter-day tribal order that he calls "The Brotherhood," in which all men would affirm their sacred loyalty to each other against the outside world. A man's position would be based on "hierarchy through meritocracy," not inherited wealth or status. All men would be expected to train and serve as warriors, and only warriors— meaning no women—would have a political voice. In this version of patriarchal ideology, unlike the Christian Right version, male comradeship is central and the family is entirely peripheral. An example of the kind of community Donovan envisions is the Odinist group Wolves of Vinland, which Donovan joined after visiting their off-the-grid community in rural Virginia in 2014. The Wolves use group rituals (including animal sacrifice) and hold fights between members to test their masculinity.[54] The Wolves of Vinland have also been praised on white nationalist websites such as *Counter-Currents Publishing*, and one of their members has been imprisoned for attempting to burn down a Black church in Virginia.[55]

Donovan has written that he is sympathetic to white nationalist aims such as encouraging racial separatism and defending European Americans against "the deeply entrenched anti-white bias of multiculturalist orthodoxies."[56] White nationalism dovetails with his beliefs that all humans are tribal creatures and human equality is an illusion. But in contrast to most alt-rightists, race is not Donovan's main focus or concern. "My work is about men. It's about understanding masculinity and the plight of men in the modern world. It's about what all men have in common." His "Brotherhood" ideal is not culturally specific and he's happy to see men of other cultures pursue similar aims. "For instance, I am not a Native American, but I

---

54. Jack Donovan, "A Time for Wolves." *Jack Donovan* (online), June 14, 2014.
55. Rose City Antifa, "The Wolves of Vinland: a Fascist Countercultural 'Tribe' in the Pacific Northwest." *Rose City Antifa* (online), November 7, 2016.
56. Jack Donovan, "Mighty White." *Jack Donovan* (online), December 18, 2011.

have been in contact with a Native American activist who read *The Way of Men* and contacted me to tell me about his brotherhood. I could never belong to that tribe, but I wish him great success in his efforts to promote virility among his tribesmen."[57]

There are strong resonances between Donovan's ideas and early fascism's violent male camaraderie, which took the intense, trauma-laced bonds that World War I veterans had formed in the trenches and transferred them into street-fighting formations such as the Italian *squadristi* and German stormtroopers. Donovan also echoes the 1909 *Futurist Manifesto*, a document that prefigured Italian Fascism: "We want to glorify war—the only cure for the world—militarism, patriotism, the destructive gesture of the anarchists, the beautiful ideas which kill, and contempt for woman."[58] Thus it's not surprising he has embraced the term "anarcho-fascism," referring to "a unified male collective ... bound together by a red ribbon of blood."[59]

In the Alternative Right and among rightists in general, the most controversial part of Donovan's ideology is that he advocates and practices "androphilia," by which he means love or sex between masculine men. Donovan doesn't call himself gay, rejects gay culture as effeminate, and justifies homophobia as a defense of masculinity rooted in the male gang's collective survival needs. His version of homosexuality is a consummation of the priority that men in his ideal gang place on each other. As he has commented, "When you get right down to it, when it comes to sex, homos are just men without women getting in the way."[60] Many Alternative Rightists consider homosexuality in any form to be immoral and a threat to racial survival, and Donovan has been vilified on many alt-right sites for his sexuality, yet his work has also won widespread support within the

57. Jack Donovan, *A Sky Without Eagles: Selected Essays and Speeches 2010–2014.* (Milwaukie, Ore.: Dissonant Hum, 2014), 166.

58. F. T. Marinetti, "The Futurist Manifesto." (1909) (online).

59. Jack Donovan, "Anarcho-Fascism." *Jack Donovan* (online), March 3, 2013.

60. Jack Donovan, Comment. *Roosh V Forum* (online), November 16, 2012.

movement. *Anti-Fascist News* has noted a broader trend among many white nationalists to include openly homosexual writers (such as James O'Meara) and musicians (such as Death in June leader Douglas Pearce), while continuing to derogate gay culture.[61]

RIGHT-WING ANARCHISTS

Like many far right currents in the United States, the alt-right offers a vision of the state that is both authoritarian and decentralist. Alt-rightists uphold classical fascism's elitist and anti-democratic views on how society should be governed, and as the movement has grown it has increasingly applauded dictatorial figures such as Augusto Pinochet.[62] At the same time, the alt-right goal of breaking up the United States into ethnically separate polities is inherently decentralist, and is rooted in both the European New Right's vision of replacing nation-states with a federated "empire" and paleoconservatism's traditional hostility to big government. The authoritarian/decentralist blend has been bolstered by two other political currents that have influenced the alt-right: right-wing anarchism and neoreaction.

As part of its project to bring together a range of dissident right-wing voices, *AlternativeRight.com* published articles by self-identified anarchists Andrew Yeoman of Bay Area National Anarchists (BANA) and Keith Preston of the website *Attack the System* (ATS). National-Anarchism, which advocates a decentralized system of "tribal" enclaves, was initiated in the

---

61. Antifascist Front, "Queer Fascism: Why White Nationalists Are Trying to Drop Homophobia." *Anti-Fascist News* (online), November 6, 2015.
62. Shane Burley, "How the Alt-Right Is Attempting to Hide Its White Supremacist Ties." *Truthout* (online), September 15, 2016.

1990s by Troy Southgate, a veteran of British neonazism.[63] Over the following years, National-Anarchist groups formed in a number of countries across Europe, the Americas, and Australia/New Zealand. The first US affiliate, BANA, began in 2007, and Southgate formally launched the National-Anarchist Movement (N-AM) in 2010.[64]

National-Anarchism is a white nationalist ideology. Like Identitarianism, it draws heavily on the ENR doctrine that ethnic and racial separatism is needed to defend so-called bio-cultural diversity. The N-AM *Manifesto* declares that race categories are basic biological facts and some people are innately superior to others. National-Anarchists also repeat classic antisemitic conspiracy theories and, like many neonazis, promote neopaganism and closeness to nature.[65] But National-Anarchists reject classical fascism for its emphasis on strong nation-states, centralized dictatorship, and collaboration with big business. Instead, they call for breaking up society into self-governing tribal communities, so that different cultures, beliefs, and practices can co-exist side by side.[66]

National-Anarchists have not had a significant presence in the Alternative Right since BANA disbanded in 2011, but self-described anarcho-pluralist Keith Preston has continued to participate in alt-right forums, for example speaking at National Policy Institute conferences and on *The Right Stuff*

63. Spencer Sunshine, "Rebranding Fascism: National-Anarchists." *The Public Eye Magazine* 23, no. 4 (2008) (online); Graham D. Macklin, "Co-opting the Counter Culture: Troy Southgate and the National Revolutionary Faction." *Patterns of Prejudice* 39, no. 3 (2005).

64. Greg Johnson, "Bay Area National Anarchists: An Interview with Andrew Yeoman, Part 1." *The Occidental Quarterly* (online), August 21, 2009; "Third Way: Introducing the National-Anarchist Movement." *National-Anarchist Movement* (online), October 3, 2010.

65. National-Anarchist Movement, "N-AM Manifesto." *National-Anarchist Movement* (2010) (online).

66. National-Anarchist Movement, "National-Anarchist Movement (N-AM) FAQ." *National-Anarchist Movement* (online), November 21, 2012.

podcasts. Preston is a former left-wing anarchist who moved to
the Right in the 1990s and then founded the group American
Revolutionary Vanguard, which is better known today by the
name of its website, *Attack the System*.[67] ATS brings together a
number of right-wing currents, including National-Anarchist,
libertarian, white nationalist, Duginist, and others, among it
editors and contributors, but Preston's own ideology is distinct
from all of these.[68]

Like the National-Anarchists, Preston advocates a decentralized, diverse network of self-governing communities, while
rejecting left-wing anarchism's commitment to dismantle social
hierarchy and oppression. Authoritarian and supremacist systems would be fully compatible with the anarcho-pluralist
model, as long as they operated on a small scale. But unlike
National-Anarchists, Preston frames his decentralist ideal in
terms of individual free choice rather than tribalism, and he is
not a white nationalist.[69] Although Preston has echoed some
racist ideas such as the claim that non-European immigrants
threaten to destroy Western civilization, his underlying philosophy is based not on race but rather a generic, Nietzschean elitism that is not ethnically specific.[70] While Preston himself is
white, several of his closest associates in the *Attack the System*
inner circle are people of color.

Preston has offered several reasons for his involvement in
the Alternative Right. He sees the movement as an important counterweight to what he calls "totalitarian humanism"

---

67. Matthew N. Lyons, "Rising Above the Herd: Keith Preston's Authoritarian
Anti-Statism." *New Politics* (online), April 29, 2011.
68. American Revolutionary Vanguard, "Statement of Purpose." *Attack the System*
(online), 2016.
69. Keith Preston, "The National-Anarchist Litmus Test." *Attack the System*
(online), April 24, 2009; Keith Preston, "The Thoughts That Guide Me." *Attack the
System* (online) (2005); Lyons 2011 op cit. (online)
70. Keith Preston, "Mass Immigration and Totalitarian Humanism." Speech at
National Policy Institute Conference, June 23, 2011 (online); Preston 2005 op cit.

(supposedly state-enforced progressive values, i.e., political correctness), he regards the alt-right's foreign policy non-interventionism and economic nationalism as superior to what the Republican or Democratic parties advocate, and he shares many alt-rightists' interest in earlier European "critics of liberal capitalism and mass democracy,"[71] meaning people like Julius Evola, Carl Schmitt, and Ernst Jünger. In addition, the alt-right allows Preston to avoid political isolation, as his efforts to reach out to left-wing anarchists have been almost completely rejected.

Preston is a respected figure within the Alternative Right, and his anti-statist vision appeals to some white national-ists in the movement. For example, *Counter-Currents* author Francisco Albanese has argued that it provides "the best and most viable option for the ethnic and racial survival" of whites in regions where they form a minority of the population. In addition, "it is only outside the state that whites can come to understand the true essence of community and construction of a common destiny."[72] At the same time, anarcho-pluralism offers potential common ground between white nationalists and other critics of the existing order, such as anarcho-capi-talists and other "market anarchists," whose ideas are regularly featured on *Attack the System*, as well as the "libertarian theo-crats" of the Christian Reconstructionist movement.[73]

Preston's approach to political strategy takes this bridge-building further. Echoing Third Position fascists, who de-

---

71. Keith Preston, "What, Exactly, is the 'Alternative Right?'" [Introductory comments.] *Attack the System* (online), December 23, 2015.
72. Francisco Albanese, "Rethinking White Tribalism: Anarchy in the Southern Cone." *Counter-Currents Publishing* (online), June 5, 2014.
73. Keith Preston, "Anarchist Economics Compared and Contrasted: Anarcho-Capitalism vs Anarcho-Syndicalism/Communism." *Attack the System* (online), March 21, 2015; Michael J. McVicar, "The Libertarian Theocrats: The Long, Strange History of R. J. Rushdoony and Christian Reconstructionism." *The Public Eye*, vol. 22, no. 3 (Fall 2007) (online).

nounce both communism and capitalism, Preston and ATS call
for a broad revolutionary alliance of all those who want to destroy US imperialism and the federal government. Within US
borders, this would involve a "pan-secessionist" strategy uniting groups across the political spectrum that want to carve out
self-governing enclaves free of US federal government control.[74]
As a step in this direction, ATS supported a series of North
American secessionist conventions, which brought together
representatives of the neo-Confederate group League of the
South, the Reconstructionist-influenced Christian Exodus,
the libertarian Free State Project, advocates of Hawaiian in-
dependence, the left-leaning Second Vermont Republic, and
others.[75]

NEOREACTION

Neoreaction is another dissident right-wing current with a
vision of small-scale authoritarianism that has emerged online
in the past decade, which overlaps with and has influenced
the Alternative Right. Like the alt-right and much of the
manosphere, neoreaction (often abbreviated as NRx, and also
known as Dark Enlightenment) is a loosely unified school of
thought that rejects egalitarianism in principle, argues that differences in human intelligence and ability are mainly genetic,
and believes that cultural and political elites wrongfully limit
the range of acceptable discourse. Blogger Curtis Yarvin (writing under the pseudonym Mencius Moldbug) first articulated
neoreactionary ideology in 2007, but many other writers have

---

74. Keith Preston, "Anarcho-Pluralism and Pan-Secessionism: What They Are and
What They Are Not." *Attack the System* (online), August 8, 2010.
75. Keith Preston, "Third North American Secessionists Convention—A Review."
Attack the System (online), November 19, 2008.

contributed to it. Neoreaction emphasizes order and restoring the social stability that supposedly prevailed before the French Revolution, along with technocratic and futurist concerns such as transhumanism, a movement that hopes to radically "improve" human beings through technology. NRx theorist Nick Land is a leading advocate of accelerationism, which in his version sees global capitalism driving ever-faster technological change, to the point that artificial intelligence essentially replaces human beings. One critic wrote that neoreaction "combines all of the awful things you always suspected about libertarianism with odds and ends from PUA culture, Victorian Social Darwinism, and an only semi-ironic attachment to absolutism. Insofar as neoreactionaries have a political project, it's to dissolve the United States into competing authoritarian seasteads on the model of Singapore…"[76]

Neoreactionaries, who are known for their arcane, verbose theoretical monologues, appear to be mostly young, computer-oriented men, and their ideas have spread partly through the tech startup scene. PayPal co-founder and Trump supporter Peter Thiel has voiced some neoreactionary-sounding ideas. In 2009, for example, he declared, "I no longer believe that freedom and democracy are compatible" and "the vast increase in welfare beneficiaries and the extension of the franchise to women…have rendered the notion of 'capitalist democracy' into an oxymoron."[77] Both Yarvin and fellow NRxer Michael Anissimov have worked for companies backed by Thiel.[78] This doesn't necessarily mean that Thiel is intentionally bankrolling the neoreactionary movement per se, but it points to resonances between that movement and Silicon Valley's larger techno-libertarian discourse.

---

76. Park MacDougald, "The Darkness Before the Right." *The Awl* (online), September 28, 2015.

77. Peter Thiel, "The Education of a Libertarian." *Cato Unbound*, April 13, 2009.

78. Klint Finley, "Geeks for Monarchy: The Rise of the Neoreactionaries." *TechCrunch* (online), November 22, 2013.

"At its heart, neoreaction is a critique of the entire liberal, politically-correct orthodoxy," commented "WhiteDeerGrotto" on the NRx blog *Habitable Worlds*. "The Cathedral, a term coined by Moldbug, is a description of the institutions and enforcement mechanisms used to propagate and maintain this orthodoxy"—a power center that consists of Ivy League and other elite universities, *The New York Times*, and some civil servants. "The politically-correct propagandists assert that humans are essentially interchangeable, regardless of culture or genetics, and that some form of multicultural social-welfare democracy is the ideal, final political state for all of humanity. Neoreaction says no. The sexes are biologically distinct, genetics matter, and democracy is deeply flawed and fundamentally unstable."[79]

While alt-rightists largely agree with these neoreactionary ideas, and some outsiders have equated the two movements, alt-right and neoreaction differ significantly. Alt-rightists might or might not invoke popular sovereignty as an achievement of European civilization, and try to strike a populist or anti-elitist pose, but neoreactionaries all regard regular people as utterly unsuited to hold political power—"a howling irrational mob" as NRx theorist Nick Land has put it.[80] Some NRxers advocate monarchy; others want to turn the state into a corporation with members of an intellectual elite as shareholders.[81] Conversely, neoreactionaries might or might not translate their genetic determinism into calls for racial solidarity, but for most alt-rightists race is the basis for everything else.[82] Unlike most alt-rightists, leading neoreactionaries have not supported

---

79. Scharlach, "Neoreaction = Monarchy?" *Habitable Worlds* (online), Nov. 23, 2013.
80. Nick Land, "The Dark Enlightenment: Part 1." *The Dark Enlightenment* (2013) (online); MacDougald op cit. (online)
81. Finley op cit. (online)
82. Hubert Collins and Hadley Bishop, "Two Prominent Identitarians Give Us Their Thoughts On Neoreaction." Interview with Michael McGregor and Gregory Hood. *Social Matter* (online), October 15, 2014.

Donald Trump.[83] In addition, while many alt-rightists emphasize antisemitism, neoreactionaries generally do not, and some neoreactionaries are Jewish or, in Yarvin's case, of mixed Jewish and non-Jewish ancestry.[84] Indeed, in *The Right Stuff*'s lexicon of alt-right terminology, "Neoreaction" translates as "Jews."

At the same time, many alt-rightists regard neoreaction as a related movement that offers many positive contributions. Some writers, such as Steve Sailer, have had a foot in both camps. Alt-rightist Gregory Hood has argued that white nationalism and neoreaction are complementary: "I've argued in the past that race is sufficient in and of itself to serve as a foundation for state policy. However, just saying that tells you very little about how precisely you execute that program. NRx and its theoretical predecessors are absolutely core to understanding how society works and how power functions."[85] Anarcho-pluralist Keith Preston applauded a proposal by NRxer Michael Anissimov to create breakaway enclaves in "low-population, defensible regions of the United States like Idaho."[86] On its own, neoreaction seems too esoteric to have much of a political impact, but its contribution to alt-right ideology might be significant.

---

83. Dylan Matthews, "The alt-right is more than warmed-over white supremacy. It's that, but way way weirder." *Vox* (online), April 18, 2016.

84. Mencius Moldbug [Curtis Yarvin], "Why I am not an anti-Semite." *Unqualified Reservations* (online), June 23, 2007.

85. Collins and Bishop op cit. (online)

86. Keith Preston, "The Growth of the Alternative Right." *Attack the System* (online), January 4, 2016.

PART 3
RELATIONSHIP WITH DONALD TRUMP

POLITICAL STRATEGY DEBATES

The Alternative Right first gained mainstream attention through its support for Donald Trump's presidential candidacy. In exploring the alt-right's relationship with the Trump campaign and with Trump as president-elect, several issues deserve special attention: the movement's debates about political strategy, its skillful use of online activism, and its attraction of a wider circle of sympathizers and popularizers who came to be known as the "alt-lite."

Alt-rightists' embrace of Trump followed several years in which they argued about whether to work within existing political channels or reject them entirely. During this period, *American Renaissance* columnnist Hubert Collins called on white nationalists to use the electoral process and ally with more mainstream anti-immigrant groups to keep whites at as high a percentage of the US population as possible.[87] In contrast, Gregory Hood of *Counter-Currents Publishing* declared that the United States was "beyond reform" and political secession was "the only way out."[88] Sidestepping this issue, many alt-rightists have followed the European New Right lead and focused on a "metapolitical" strategy of seeking to transform the broader culture. In Lawrence Murray's words, "When the idea of White nationalism has taken root among enough of our people, the potential to demand, demonstrate, and act will be superior to what it currently is."[89] Jack Donovan has argued

87. Anti-Defamation League, "Point of Contention: A Fractured White Supremacist Take on Immigration." *Anti-Defamation League* (online), May 5, 2015.
88. Gregory Hood. "The Solution is State Power." *Counter-Currents Publishing* (online), December 2012.
89. Lawrence Murray, "White Nationalism FAQ." *The Right Stuff* (online), April 14, 2016.

that the US is on the road to becoming a failed state and urged alt-rightists to "build the kinds of resilient communities and networks of skilled people that can survive the collapse and preserve your identities after the Fall."[90] To Donovan, this is an optimistic scenario: "In a failed state, we go back to Wild West rules, and America becomes a place for men again—a land full of promise and possibility that rewards daring and ingenuity, a place where men can restart the world."[91]

Whether or not to work within established political channels has been debated at movement events, with some alt-rightists moving from one position to another. Richard Spencer, for example, argued in 2011 that "the GOP could unite a substantial majority of white voters by focusing its platform on immigration restriction." This strategy "would...ensure that future Americans inherit a country that resembles that of their ancestors."[92] But two years later, Spencer seemingly turned his back on the Republican Party and called for creating a separate white ethnostate in North America. He declared, "the majority of children born in the United States are non-White. Thus, from our perspective, any future immigration-restriction efforts are meaningless." Spencer also argued that "restoring the Constitution," (going back to an aristocratic republic run by property-owning white men) as some white nationalists advocated, would only lead to a similar or worse situation.[93]

One approach has been to propose working within the system in order to weaken it, advocating changes that sound reasonable but require radical change—a right-wing version

---

90. Jack Donovan, "Becoming the New Barbarians." *Radix* (online), December 23, 2013.

91. Jack Donovan, "The Bright Side of Illegal Immigration." *Jack Donovan* (online), November 13, 2012.

92. Richard Spencer, "The Majority Strategy: The Essential Argument—Why The GOP Must Win White America," *V-Dare* (online), September 8, 2011.

93. Richard Spencer, "Facing the Future as a Minority," *The National Policy Institute* (online) April 30, 2013.

of the Trotskyist transitional demand strategy. Ted Sallis, for example, urged white nationalists to "demand a seat at the multicultural table, represented by *real* advocates of White interests, not groveling patsies." This would involve using the language of multiculturalism to complain about "legitimate" cases of discrimination against whites or members of other dominant groups. The aim here would not be "reforming the System. It is instead using the contradictions and weaknesses of the System against itself…"[94]

To a large extent, Alternative Rightist support for Trump's presidential candidacy followed a related approach of using the system against itself. Alt-rightists began praising Trump in 2015, and by mid-2016 most of the movement was applauding him. But this support was qualified by the recognition that Trump was not one of them and was not going to bring about the change they wanted. Brad Griffin, who blogs at *Occidental Dissent* under the name Hunter Wallace, hoped in late 2015 that Trump "provokes a fatal split that topples the GOP."[95] The Traditionalist Youth Network declared:

> "While Donald Trump is neither a Traditionalist nor a White nationalist, he is a threat to the economic and social powers of the international Jew. For this reason alone as long as Trump stands strong on deportation and immigration enforcement we should support his candidacy insofar as we can use it to push more hardcore positions on immigration and Identity. Donald Trump is not the savior of Whites in America, he is however a booming salvo across the bow of the Left and Jewish

94. Ted Sallis, "Democratic Multiculturalism: Strategy & Tactics." *Counter-Currents Publishing* (online), November 19, 2014.
95. Hunter Wallace [Brad Griffin], "Trump, White Nationalists, The Media." *Occidental Dissent*, December 10, 2015. Comment by Hunter Wallace, December 10, 2015 at 8:53 pm. (archived at http://bit.ly/fatalsplit)

power to tell them that White America is awakening,
and we are tired of business as usual."[96]

At *The Right Stuff*, "Professor Evola-Hitler" argued that Trump
had broken important taboos on issues such as curtailing
immigration and ending birthright citizenship, damaged the
Republican Party's pro-Israel coalition, shifted the party closer
to ethnic nationalism, and "offers the opportunity for the alt-
right to expand quickly," but cautioned that "We need to be taking advantage of Trump, not allow Trump to take advantage
of us."[97]

Not all alt-rightists supported Trump. *The Right Stuff*
contributor "Auschwitz Soccer Ref" argued that alt-rightists
shouldn't support Trump since two of his children had mar-
ried Jews, making him "naturally loyal" to Israel.[98] Jack Donovan
suggested that a Hillary Clinton presidency would be prefer-
able, because she would "drive home the reality that white men
are no longer in charge...and that [the United States] is no
longer their country and never will be again,"[99] Keith Preston
commented, "The alt-right's attachment to Trump seems to
be a mirror image repeat of the religious right's attachment
to Reagan, i.e. the case of an insurgent, somewhat reactionary,
populist movement being taken for a ride by a thoroughly pro-
ruling class centrist politician motivated primarily by personal
ambition."[100] However, these anti-Trump voices were squarely
in the minority.

---

96. Traditionalist Youth Network, "The Trump Train and the Southern Strategy:
The Only Hope for the GOP." *Traditionalist Youth Network* (online), October 2015.
97. Professor Evola-Hitler, "Trump's Our Guy for the 2016 Election. We Have No
Choice." *The Right Stuff* (online), April 29, 2016.
98. Auschwitz Soccer Ref, "Trump's Not Our Guy. It's Time to Stop Pretending
Otherwise." *The Right Stuff* (online), April 25, 2016.
99. Jack Donovan, "No One Will Ever Make America Great Again." *Jack Donovan*
(online), July 7, 2016.
100. Keith Preston, "The Alternative Right—An Autopsy." *Attack the System*
(online), May 21, 2016.

INTERNET MEMES
AND HARASSMENT CAMPAIGNS

The main way that alt-rightists helped Trump's campaign was through online activism. A pivotal example came in the summer of 2015, when alt-rightists promoted the #cuckservative meme to attack Trump's GOP rivals as traitors and sellouts to liberalism. "Cuckservative" combines the words "conservative" and "cuckold," meaning a man whose wife has sex with other men. As journalist Joseph Bernstein pointed out, "The term's connotations are racist. By alluding to a genre of porn in which passive white husbands watch their wives have sex with black men, it casts its targets as impotent defenders of white people in America."[101] During the weeks leading up to the first Republican presidential debate, alt-rightists spread the meme across social media to boost Trump and vilify his GOP rivals, as in a Tweet that showed a picture of Jeb Bush with the words, "Please fuck my country, Mexico. #Cuckservative."[102] As *Anti-Fascist News* pointed out, this initiative "allowed racialist discourse to shift into the public, making #cuckservative an accusation that mainstream Republicans feel like they have to answer to."[103]

Alt-rightists also turned online harassment and abuse into a potent tactic for frightening and silencing opponents, borrowing directly from the manosphere's Gamergate campaign discussed above. In the Spring of 2016, for example, anti-Trump protesters at Portland State University were flooded with racist, transphobic, and antisemitic messages, doxxing, and rape and death threats, sent from anonymous social media accounts. Reflecting the manosphere's influence, alt-right harassment

---

101. Joseph Bernstein, "Behind The Racist Hashtag That Is Blowing Up Twitter." *BuzzFeed* (online), July 27, 2015.
102. Ibid.
103. Antifascist Front (2015), "#Cuckservative" op cit. (online)

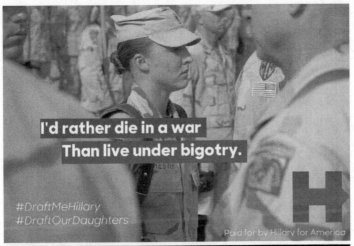

Memes such as the above have become one of the main tools of alt-right propaganda on the internet, to the point that the term "meme magic" has been coined to vaunt their effectiveness in bringing about change.

often emphasized sexual violence and the humiliation of women and girls, even when men were the supposed targets.[104] David French, staff writer at the conservative *National Review*, described the year-long stream of relentless online abuse his family has endured because he criticized Trump and the alt-right:

> *"I saw images of my daughter's face in gas chambers, with a smiling Trump in a Nazi uniform preparing to press a button and kill her. I saw her face photoshopped into images of slaves. She was called a 'niglet' and a 'dindu.' The alt-right unleashed on my wife, Nancy, claiming that she had slept with black men while I was deployed to Iraq, and that I loved to watch while she had sex with 'black bucks.' People sent her pornographic images of black men having sex with white women, with someone photoshopped to look like me, watching."[105]*

Another example of alt-right online activism was the campaign to "wedge gays and Muslims," as "Butch Leghorn" of *The Right Stuff* put it. Writing in June 2016, two days after Afghani American Omar Mateen murdered 49 people at a gay nightclub in Orlando, Florida, Leghorn declared, "Gays will never be safe from Muslim violence, and the liberals will allow Muslim violence against gays because Muslims are higher ranked on the Progressive stack than gays…. This makes [the Orlando] shooting a very valuable wedge issue. By allowing Muslims into America, the Democrats are in effect choosing Muslims over gays. We simply need to hammer this issue. Meme magic is real boys, so spread this meme. Drive this wedge. Smash

---

104. Robert Evans, "5 Things You Learn Being Attacked By The Alt-Right." *Cracked* (online), September 20, 2016.

105. David French, "The Price I've Paid for Opposing Donald Trump." *National Review* (online), October 21, 2016.

their coalition."[106] Leghorn offered several examples of talking points and images to use, such as a rainbow flag with the words "Fuck Islam" superimposed over it.

One of the alt-right's most skillful uses of social media in 2016 was the #DraftOurDaughters meme, which was trending on Twitter the week before the election. As the website *Know Your Meme* explained, "#DraftOurDaughters is a satirical social media hashtag launched by supporters of Donald Trump which encourages American women to register for Selective Service in preparation for hypothetical scenarios of United States military operations that would supposedly be launched by Hillary Clinton if she were elected as President of the United States." The campaign included a series of fake Clinton campaign ads, many of which feature images of women in military uniform and slogans such as "Hillary will stand up to Russian Aggression. Will you stand with her?," "I'd rather die in a war than live under bigotry," and "In the White House or on Russian soil. The fight for equality never stops."[107]

#DraftOurDaughters portrayed the Clinton campaign as fusing feminism/multiculturalism and aggressive militarism. Since that was a reasonably accurate description of Clinton's politics, the meme was equally effective as either disinformation or satire. A number of alt-right sites, such as *Vox Popoli* and *The Daily Stormer*, promoted the campaign.[108] Along with spreading the "ads" themselves, alt-rightists also spread the phony claim that mainstream media had been taken in by them.[109]

---

106. Butch Leghorn, "Wedging Gays and Muslims," *The Right Stuff* (online), June 14, 2016.

107. Know Your Meme. N.d. "#DraftOurDaughters." *Know Your Meme* (online).

108. Eric Striker, "#DraftOurDaughters: Feminist Hillary Supporters Vow to Fight War With Russia For Us." *The Daily Stormer* (online), October 28, 2016; Vox Day [Theodore Beale], "Draft our Daughters." *Vox Popoli* (online), Oct. 28, 2016.

109. Abby Ohlheiser, "What was fake on the Internet this election: #DraftOurDaughters, Trump's tax returns." *The Washington Post* (online), October 31, 2016.

THE ALT-LITE

As the alt-right has grown and attracted increased attention, it has also developed complicated relationships with more moderate rightists. The movement has largely defined itself and drawn energy by denouncing conservatives, and some conservatives have returned the favor, such as the prestigious *National Review*.[110] At the same time, other conservatives have taken on the role of apologists or supporters for the alt-right, helping to spread a lot of its message without embracing its full ideology or its ethnostate goals. Richard Spencer and his comrades began to call this phenomenon the "alt-right-lite" or simply the "alt-lite." Alt-rightists have relied on the alt-lite to help bring their ideas to a mass, mainstream audience, but to varying degrees they have also regarded alt-lite figures with resentment, as ideologically untrustworthy opportunists.

Breitbart News Network is the preeminent example of alt-lite politics. Founded in 2007, *Breitbart* featured sensationalist attacks on liberals and liberal groups, praise for the Tea Party's anti-big government populism, and aggressive denials that conservatives were racist, sexist, or homophobic. Under Steve Bannon, who took over leadership in 2012, the organ began to scapegoat Muslims and immigrants more directly.[111] In March 2016, *Breitbart* published "An Establishment Conservative's Guide to the Alt-Right," by Allum Bokhari and Milo Yiannopoulos, which asserted—without evidence—that most alt-rightists did not believe their own racist propaganda, but were actually just libertarians trying to shock people.[112] The article helped boost the alt-right's profile and acceptability

110. Ian Tuttle, "The Racist Moral Rot at the Heart of the Alt-Right." *National Review* (online), April 5, 2016.

111. Stephen Piggott, "Is Breitbart.com Becoming the Media Arm of the 'Alt-Right'?" *Hatewatch* (online), April 28, 2016. *Southern Poverty Law Center*.

112. Allum Bokhari and Milo Yiannopoulos, "An Establishment Conservative's Guide to the Alt-Right." *Breitbart* (online), March 29, 2016.

in mainstream circles, yet many alt-rightists criticized it for glossing over their white nationalist ideology.[113]

Over the following months, Yiannopoulos—a flamboyantly gay man of Jewish descent and a political performer who vilifies Muslims and women and refers to Donald Trump as "Daddy"—became publicly identified with the alt-right himself, to mixed reviews from alt-rightists.[114] Meanwhile, Steve Bannon declared *Breitbart* "the platform of the alt-right" and began publishing semi-veiled antisemitic attacks on Trump's opponents, all while insisting that white nationalists, antisemites, and homophobes were marginal to the alt-right.[115] Richard Spencer was pleased when Donald Trump hired Bannon to run his campaign, commenting that "Breitbart has acted as a 'gateway' to Alt Right ideas and writers" and that the media outlet "has people on board who take us seriously, even if they are not Alt Right themselves."[116] But other alt-rightists have been more critical of the alt-lite phenomenon. At *Occidental Dissent*, Brad Griffin describes the alt-lite as "basically conservative websites pushing Alt-Right material in order to generate clicks and revenue," and asks, "What the hell does Milo Yiannopoulos—a Jewish homosexual who boasts about carrying on interracial relationships with black men—have to do with us?"[117]

113. Antifascist Front, "Going Full Fash: Breitbart Mainstreams the 'Alt Right.'" *Anti-Fascist News* (online), April 5, 2016.

114. Antifascist Front, "Meet the Alt Lite, the People Mainstreaming the Alt Right's White Nationalism." *Anti-Fascist News* (online), November 3, 2016.

115. Sarah Posner, "How Donald Trump's New Campaign Chief Created an Online Haven for White Nationalists." *Mother Jones* (online), August 22, 2016; Michelle Goldberg, "*Breitbart* Calls Trump Foe 'Renegade Jew.' This Is How Anti-Semitism Goes Mainstream." *Slate* (online), May 16, 2016.

116. Richard B. Spencer, "Make Trump Trump Again." *Radix* (online), August 17, 2016.

117. Hunter Wallace [Brad Griffin], "Alt-Right vs. Alt-Lite." *Occidental Dissent* (online), November 23, 2016.

CONCLUSION
THE ALT-RIGHT AND THE TRUMP PRESIDENCY

Most alt-rightists were thrilled by Trump's upset victory over Hillary Clinton, but not because they believe that Trump shares their politics or will bring about the changes that they want. Rather, they believe a Trump presidency will offer them "breathing room" to promote their ideology and to "move the Overton window" in their favor.[118] In turn, they see themselves as the Trump coalition's political vanguard, taking hardline positions that pull Trump further to the right while enabling him to look moderate by comparison. In Richard Spencer's words, "The Alt Right and Trumpian populism are now aligned much in the way the Left is aligned with Democratic politicians like Obama and Hillary.... We—*and only we*— can say the things Trump can't say ... can criticize him in the right way ... and can envision a new world that he can't quite grasp."[119] The Traditionalist Youth Network was more specific: "We cannot and will not back down on the Jewish Question or our explicit racial identity. We won't. Don't worry. But we will join those who aren't as radical as we are in pulling politics in our direction."[120]

But the question of how to play that vanguard role has already sharpened tensions between the alt-right and its sympathizers, and to some extent within the alt-right itself. At the National Policy Institute conference shortly after the election, Spencer's closing speech ended with the shout "Hail Trump, hail our people, hail victory!" which many audience members

---

118. Vox Day [Theodore Beale], "Trumpslide!" *Vox Popoli* (online), November 9, 2016; James Dunphy, "It's Time to Turn Up the Heat." *Counter-Currents Publishing* (online), November 2016.

119. Richard B. Spencer, "We the Vanguard Now." *Radix* (online), November 9, 2016.

120. Matt Parrott, "Trump Apocalypse Now." *Traditionalist Youth Network* (online), November 2016.

greeted with fascist salutes. The fact that it was caught on video by journalists made it a politically embarrassing moment. Alt-lite figure Mike Cernovich claimed, absurdly, that Spencer had acted on behalf of the government to deliberately discredit the movement. Several other sympathizers, and even long-time alt-rightist Greg Johnson of *Counter-Currents*, also criticized Spencer's behavior as damaging.[121]

In the months and years ahead, there are likely to be further tensions within the larger Trump coalition, which spans from alt-rightists to mainstream conservatives. Although Trump's choice of Steve Bannon as chief strategist and senior counselor puts someone with alt-right ties close to the center of power, most of his other appointments are hardline establishment figures. On a number of issues, from immigration policy to Israel, alt-rightists could easily find themselves pushed into an oppositional role. vdare.com founder Peter Brimelow has warned that alt-rightists might "revolt" if the Trump administration fails to move in the direction they want.[122]

Even if that happens, however, alt-rightists could continue to exert significant pressure on a Trump administration, because they know how to speak effectively to a large part of his popular base. The alt-right has helped revitalize white nationalist and male supremacist politics in the United States. While earlier generations of far right activists broke new ground with online bulletin boards such as *Stormfront*, alt-rightists have made effective use of the internet for everything from theoretical debate to mass campaigns of targeted ridicule. In previous decades, white nationalists largely relied on coded language and euphemisms when seeking mass support, but alt-rightists often parade their hate ideology aggressively and confidently.

121. Antifascist Front, "Let's Watch as the Alt Right Implodes." *Anti-Fascist News* (online), December 4, 2016.

122. Rory Carroll, "'Alt-right' groups will 'revolt' if Trump shuns white supremacy, leaders say." *The Guardian* (online), December 27, 2016.

Although the movement has seen its share of infighting, it has also been relatively successful in crafting a workable "big-tent" culture that welcomes diverse points of view and fosters fruitful interchange with related ideological currents.

The alt-right has been buoyed by Donald Trump's drive to the presidency, and has aided Trump in return, while maintaining a clear sense of the relationship's limits. Unlike many grassroots initiatives that pour themselves into electoral politics and get trapped, the alt-right is well positioned to maintain its own identity and freedom of maneuver. Because it mostly exists online, the alt-right does not have the infrastructure needed to launch a guerrilla war (as Nazi/Klan forces did in the 1980s) or build pseudo-state institutions (as Patriot groups did in the 1990s, and are attempting again now), but it is in a strong position to pursue a "metapolitical" transformation of the political culture and thereby lay the groundwork for structural change, centered on its vision of a white ethnostate.

THE RICH KIDS OF FASCISM

Why The Alt-Right Didn't Start With Trump, and Won't End With Him Either

It's Going Down

It seems like every time we turn on the TV, look on social media, or read a newspaper, we hear about the growth of a "movement" that doesn't even really exist outside of the internet—*the alt-right*. The media, it would seem, won't be satisfied until a *physical* fascist movement on the streets actually *does appear*. To paraphrase something Hitler said jokingly, democracy often paves the way for fascists to destroy it. But while reporters go gaga over "fashy haircuts," explain what it means to be "red-pilled," and roll out the red carpet for meme culture, the real lessons of the alt-right are largely being lost on everyone; even those that want an end to the current system of domination and physically oppose its fascist defenders.

As the latest incarnation of the white supremacist movement in the US, the alt-right signals a change in strategy *and* ideology for American fascists and white nationalists. It signals a turn away from former positions on gender and class, and toward a constituency that is more educated, urban, and upper class. Anarchists and anti-fascists need to take stock of these changes and differences, understand the ideas and strategy that drive the alt-right, and organize accordingly.

We need to understand that this divergence from previous generations (and in some cases, current ones) will cause
strife and division within the white nationalist movement as a
whole. At a time when white nationalists are calling for "unity"
in their circles like never before, the alt-right is rife with tensions as jealousy, backbiting, name calling, and denunciations
of individuals and groups run rampant. This reality can been
seen most clearly in the wake of the recent National Policy
Institute conference, where several attendees gave the Nazi
salute as MC Richard Spencer screamed, "Hail Trump!" The
resulting media fallout sent several prominent white nationalists running to the hills, only to quickly disavow themselves of
their former comrades in the press, throwing decades of connections and projects under the bus.[1] Ironic, that a subculture
so famously built on podcasts laced with the "n word" and gas
chamber memes could become so embarrassed with itself for
its behavior.

But while white supremacists like Richard Spencer are now
given airtime on a variety of programs like stupid pet tricks,
many in the media have been keen on the notion that Trump
himself inspired the creation of the alt-right and that his election has unleashed with it a flood of far right mobilization
by his existence alone. While it is true that Trump's electoral
win has unleashed a flood of violence, this is a reality that has
been playing out for over a year, and is itself a reaction to other
developments. Furthermore, such logic follows, that if Trump
fades, so will his white nationalist auxiliary forces. This con-
ception is an utter mistake.

The alt-right is much more dangerous than a reserve
Twitter army of angry men posting memes of Pepe the Frog,
wearing red Trump hats while harassing women and people
of color from the safety of their mom's basement. It was, and

---

1. Serge F. Kovaleski, Julie Turkewitz, Joseph Goldstein and Dan Barry, "An Alt-
Right Makeover Shrouds the Swastikas." *New York Times* (online), Dec. 10, 2016.

is, a growing collection of people, that while currently acting as an auxiliary force for the Trump regime is poised to become, if it continues to evolve, more of a potentially street based and "revolutionary" movement. Its origins have more to do with the white reactionary pushback against the Ferguson Insurrection, feminism, the transgender movement, and Black Lives Matter, than simply *just* the Trump campaign. If it does continue, which it is sure to do, it will predictably splinter around questions of violence, electoralism, and class. What comes next will predictably be much more horrifying.

We as anti-fascists and revolutionary anarchists need to be confident in our own strengths and not feed into the media-generated hype around the alt-right. By and large, the alt-right hasn't been able to turn into a physical movement on the streets, *yet*. They don't have offices, community centers, bookstores, publications, organizations, and unions like we do, *yet*. What the alt-right has is mainstream media hype, a tiny amount of influence in the Trump regime, and a sea of potential supporters that could also swing in other directions; but not yet a *movement*.

The hype around the alt-right is speculative, much like our economy. And, just like the housing market, at some point it's going to burst. It is much like in 1997 when *Spin Magazine* argued that techno was going to be the new grunge; and it didn't take long before everyone realized that this wasn't going to be true. Now, in 2017, we need to remind ourselves of this reality again. The media does not create movements; it creates hype. The alt-right is this year's Y2K. We need to suss out reality from the hype while coming to grip with the real challenges we face with this new and strange opponent.

Furthermore, we need to come to terms with the media spotlight put on the alt-right and what it means, as well as understand that due to the nature and makeup of *our movement*, we will *never* be given similar treatment. Lastly, we must attack this notion that the alt-right is simply a reaction to, or a part of, the Trump phenomenon. Instead, *like* Trump, the alt-right is an *elitist* reaction to popular movements from below that seek to challenge systems of power and exploitation while *molding* support for authoritarian populism and fascism among the broader population.

OUT OF THE SAFE SPACE OF THE INTERNET

The alt-right is a collection of ideological tendencies, groups, websites, podcasts, think-tanks, internet cultures, and talking heads that have created a new breed of white supremacist within the millennial generation. While they disown this term, their ideology is based on the concept that biologically, white people living in America of European origin are different from all others. White people, according to the alt-right, are biologically smarter, less prone to crime, and more akin to build "great civilizations" than human beings that are not.

For reasons of demography, many have left behind the old dream of purging all non-whites, and now instead settle on the creation of "white ethnostates" which would be politically organized along fascist lines. There is much disagreement as to the size of such states and how non-whites would be removed from their borders and placed into their own homeland/reservation, or according to some, completely removed and "sent back" to their land of origin. Thus, while choosing to label themselves Identitarians, white nationalists, race realists, or national socialists, the point remains that for them, the superiority of the white race requires the creation of a separate state and the physical exclusion of non-whites. Moreover, the resulting fascist authoritarian system would also exclude Jews, by and large homosexuals (at least from public life), Leftists, feminists, and anarchists of all stripes, and crush dissent and revolt.

But this new crop of reactionaries is by and large seemingly divorced from the old-guard of previous generations of neonazis, KKK groups, Holocaust Deniers, far right racist militias, and white power skinheads. While there is some overlap, there are more differences which separate the two scenes, and there is also a growing division between the more "traditionalist" brand of white supremacists and the alt-right. These differences hinge more on targets of recruitment, bases of operation, class positions, aesthetics and rhetoric used, views on women and homosexuality, political positioning, and where the two camps place their energies through action and propaganda.[2]

This division in the white nationalist movement is becoming more and more clear. On one side stand those that wish to continue on from where the old guard left off: the American Nazi Party, David Duke, various KKK formations, Tom Metzger of White Aryan Resistance, Aryan Nations and the Creativity Movement which sought to meld supremacist ideas with religion, and many more. The continuation of this camp can best be seen in the National Socialist Movement (NSM) and the Traditionalist Worker Party/Youth Network (TWP/TYN), headed by 25 year-old Matthew Heimbach. These two groups have recently formed the Nationalist Alliance, have begun working with skinhead gangs and KKK groups, and the NSM has even moved to stop publically displaying the swastika. By and large, these groups are (at least partially) rurally based, and present themselves as the vanguard of the white working class, and in doing so deploy a "third positionist" language that often comes across as Leftist. For instance, TWP banners read: "100% Socialist, 100% Nationalist." While obviously this marks them as National Socialist (i.e., the National Socialist German Workers Party, or Nazis), for many people, that fact will simply go over their heads.

---

2. Antifascist Front, "Queer Fascism: Why White Nationalists Are Trying To Drop Homophobia." *Anti-Fascist News* (online), November 6, 2016.

But while the harbingers of the old guard in rural areas gather together for neonazi skinhead concerts and cross lighting ceremonies, in the cities, DC think-tanks, universities, and upper-class fraternities, another section of the movement is growing: the alt-right.

ANALYSIS OF A MOVEMENT, POINT BY POINT

The alt-right exists on different organizational and political levels:

▶ Think-tanks, book publishers, and pseudo-academic conferences and journals help to give the movement a set of ideological leaders, media spokespeople, and a shared ideology. This includes the American Renaissance headed by Jared Taylor; VDARE, an anti-immigrant website and think-tank which is fronted by Peter Brimelow; *Counter-Currents Publishing* that is headed by Greg Johnson; and the National Policy Institute (NPI) led by Richard Spencer, who coined the term, "Alternative Right." NPI also produces the *Radix* journal and sells books online. These groups, projects, and people constitute an ideological leadership as well as a liaison to the mainstream media which has been crucial to their growth in exposure.

▶ Podcasts, websites, and internet culture act as a vehicle for communication for the alt-right as well as a means in which ideas can crosspollinate without being attacked. The biggest and most influential of these have been *The Right Stuff* (TRS) podcast network, the neonazi news website, *The Daily Stormer*, which produces "news" and podcasts, and Red Ice Radio, which moved from concentrating on conspiracy theories into full blown neonazism. In many ways, the internet represents the only place left that white supremacists can go and congregate without fear of being confronted. Thus, in *Reddit* groups, on *4chan*, on Twitter, and through podcasts, a subculture has been nurtured and is now attempting to grow out of just being confined to online spaces.

▶ Activist organizations such as Identity Evropa, American Vanguard, Portland Students for Trump, and more. As the alt-right has grown online, it has attempted to push away from the confines of the internet. Some groups have attempted to construct themselves as an alt-right force on the streets; these currently largely consist of Identity Evropa, which outreaches to middle to upper-middle class males in college, American Vanguard, which is largely a more aesthetically neonazi version of IE, and various alt-right groups that have supported Trump, such as the Portland Students for Trump.

The things that make the alt-right different from previous waves and formations of white supremacists are:

▶ They reject by and large a pseudo class analysis, and more or less any pandering to the "white working class." They are more interested in reaching out to college-educated, urban-based, and financially secure men than rural, poor, or working-class people. In short, the alt-right, speaking in terms of race, gender, and class—*is an elitist movement.* Moreover, they attempt to appeal to white men who react negatively to social movements that challenge systems of white supremacy and patriarchy within society. For the alt-right, the threat isn't to *white workers* but instead to *white-ness* as a social position and caste within the American system. The failure of neoliberalism and statecraft in the US so far as they're concerned is that the dominant State system has failed to uphold these racial, gendered, and class hierarchies and thus has been made irrelevant (the alt-right cites the end of Jim Crow and changing immigration laws as part of this failure). The only solution for them is an entirely new system: fascism and ethno-nationalism. They propose that any problems that white workers or the poor face now will be fixed and corrected once a fascist ethnostate is created, or as *The Daily Stormer* writes, "If we were to physically remove Jews, however, [things] would probably fall into place naturally." Lastly, it should also be stated that by and large the alt-right is made up of men from upper-middle class backgrounds, many of whom went to private schools, prestigious universities, who were enrolled in up-scale fraternities, and so on; Richard Spencer being a shining example. While alt-rightists see themselves as "dapper," to the majority of people they appear to be exactly what they are: *rich kids*. The alt-right's elitist position is best articulated by Greg Johnson of *Counter-Currents* in the essay "New Right vs Old Right":

> "[W]e need to adopt a resolutely elitist strategy. We need to recognize that, culturally and politically speaking, some whites matter more than others. History is not made by the masses. It is made out of the masses. It is made by elites molding the masses. Thus we need to direct our message to the educated, urban middle and professional classes and above."

▶ The alt-right doesn't care about women and sees them politically, like poor or working-class whites, as essentially non-actors. While there are some alt-right women, such as Lana Lokteff from Red Ice Radio, these women are simply exceptions to the rule. Furthermore, there continues to be more and more cross-over with the "manosphere" and Men's Rights Activists (MRAs), who essentially take the argument the alt-right makes about races being fundamentally unequal and *different* and applies it to gender. Well-known MRA writers such as Roosh V (who argued that rape should be legalized on private property owned by men) and Matt Forney (who looks and acts like every "SJW" the far right mocks) have continued to cross into the white nationalist camp, speaking at NPI events and working with Red Ice Radio. The internet has also helped to funnel a lot of people from the manosphere into the alt-right, through things like #Gamergate which harassed women online and threatened them with rape and violence, and propelled the career of "alt-lite" personality Milo Yiannopoulos. As Matthew Lyons has pointed out, in many ways, this flies in the face of the "separate but equal" stance of many white nationalists who often applauded the contributions of women to fascist movements.[3] Here, Matt Forney sums up the alt-right's position on women in the *Chicago Tribune*:

> "*Trying to 'appeal' to women is an exercise in pointlessness.... it's not that women should be unwelcome [in the alt-right], it's that they're unimportant.*"

▶ The alt-right is antisemitic and considers Jews to be a separate race from whites, by and large denies the Holocaust, but also normalizes and laughs about the wholesale slaughter of Jews and non-whites. Furthermore, they view Jews as having a negative impact on white people throughout history. While this borrows much from obvious sham conspiracy documents such as *The Protocols of the Elders of Zion*, the current articulation of this position is best put forward by the professor Kevin MacDonald who speaks regularly

---

3. Matthew Lyons, "Alt-right: more misogynistic than many neonazis." *Three Way Fight* (online), December 3, 2016.

at various alt-right conferences, as well as alt-right websites such as *The Daily Stormer*, who wrote in their intro to the alt-right:

> "*The defining value of the [alt-right] movement and the foundation of its ideology is that the Jews are fundamentally opposed to the White race and Western civilization and so must be confronted and ultimately removed from White societies completely.*"

▶ Another central pillar to the alt-right's worldview is that (in their view) it can be scientifically proven that there are biological differences in race and that this corresponds with levels of intelligence, a person's tendency to act in criminal or anti-social ways, a person's ability to create and maintain "civilizations," and in the case of Jews, the belief that they are genetically prone to destroy "white" civilizations and negatively affect them. Thus, the foundation for a rational society should be inequality recognizing the "superiority" of whites. As Richard Spencer wrote:

> "*A century and a half ago, Alexander Stephens, Vice-President of the Confederate States of America, was faced with the prospect of the victory or annihilation of his nation and fledgling state in what is now referred to as the American Civil War.*

> "*In his greatest address, 'The Cornerstone of the Confederacy,' he did not speak (mendaciously) about 'states rights' or any kind of Constitutional legality. He instead cut to the heart of the social order he was opposing. He stressed that the Confederacy was based on the conclusion that Thomas Jefferson was wrong; the 'cornerstone' of the new state was the 'physical, philosophical, and moral truth' of human inequality.*

> *"Ours, too, should be a declaration of difference and distance—'We hold these truths to be self-evident; that all men are created unequal.' In the wake of the old world, this will be our proposition."*[4]

▶ The use of terms and talking points taken from "identity politics," turned towards their own ends.

▶ Lastly, according to the alt-right, all those that oppose them (and other white nationalists of all stripes), are in fact protectors of the dominant political and economic order, essentially "work for the Jews," and act as defenders of both neoliberal corporate capitalism and "communism."

The enemies of the alt-right should take note of these differences if they are to destroy it.

GROWING REACTION TO BLACK REVOLT AND POPULAR MOVEMENTS

The increase of both the alt-right and a new wave of neonazi, KKK, and general white nationalist action, violence, waves of vandalism, and more was part of a growing *reaction* to the Ferguson Insurrection and the Black Lives Matter movement, not simply a consequence of the Trump campaign. This growth post-Ferguson has impacted all aspects of the far right. As Shane Bauer wrote for *Mother Jones* after having gone undercover in one such group, the 3%ers:

---

4. "Big Nazi On Campus: How Well Dressed Racists Are Coming to a College Near You." *It's Going Down* (online), May 15, 2016.

> "A Marine veteran and IT manager from Colorado
> named Mike Morris, known here as Fifty Cal, felt
> that if threepers were going to restore the Constitution,
> they needed to be organized and well trained. In 2013,
> he founded 3UP and became its commanding officer.
> Membership 'exploded' after the Ferguson protests, he
> says. He boasts that the 3UP's Colorado branch, its larg-
> est, now has 3,400 members."[5]

As we wrote in *Bern Notice*:

> "In the past year, we have seen this play out in the streets
> several times. In Olympia, we watched as Neo-Nazi
> skinheads took to the streets in support of the police. In
> Minneapolis, white nationalist members of the Patriot
> movement (and Trump supporters), fired upon dem-
> onstrators during the #JusticeforJamar occupation. In
> Seattle, members of the Hammerskin Nation attempted
> to march in a predominantly queer neighborhood.
> Moreover, in the face of almost a total media blackout, a
> wave of arson attacks against black churches was carried
> out throughout the South. In short, the far-right has hit
> the streets more in the last two years than they have since
> the 1990s. It's also important to note that in all of these
> instances, as it was in Anaheim, it took people physically
> confronting them to drive them out."[6]

Since the time of that writing, we have seen attempted large
scale far right mobilizations in Sacramento which led to violent clashes, shutdowns of the KKK in North Carolina, raucous

---

5. Shane Bauer, "Undercover with a Border Militia." *Mother Jones* (online),
November/December 2016.
6. "Bern Notice: Building A Material Force in the Age of Trumpism." *It's Going
Down* (online), March 4, 2016.

protests outside of NPI's conference in Washington DC, disruptions and protests of Milo's latest speaking tour, and more.

It is important to remember that the growth of the far right as a whole in the current period is a grassroots reactionary pushback against all popular movements from below, and this reality follows similar trajectories to the past. In 2006, as the immigrant rights movement grew and took to the streets, in reaction the militia and white nationalist movements swelled as armed gangs of men headed to the border to police "illegals."

Going back farther still, some of the earliest postwar American Nazis such as George Rockwell and the American Nazi Party grew to be their most influential when they intervened in protests against attempts to integrate housing in suburbs outside Chicago as well as decrying "race-mixing" as a conspiracy of Jewish communists. And going back even farther still, organizations such as the KKK were created in order to use terror to enforce the subjugation of black workers that generated massive amounts of wealth for the white land-owning aristocracy. But this terror quickly grew to include other targets, as the KKK soon went after radicals, union organizers, and white people that pushed back against the Klan.

Back to present day, we are also seeing beyond just the Trump campaign and anti-immigrant circles, another "crossover" issue growing around Blue Lives Matter, as many reactionary elements seek to support the police who are (sometimes literally) coming under fire as thousands rise up against continued police murders and brutality. This drive to support and defend the police who are being fought against by grassroots movements, from Chicago to North Dakota, is of course being supported by a wide range of white nationalists.

To overlook the role that reaction to popular movements, especially black revolt, plays in feeding into far right movements does a disservice to understanding fascism in the present day and white supremacy more broadly.

THE ALT-RIGHT AND TRUMP

As the grassroots autonomous far right has fed off of the white reaction to black insurrection and the growing power of social movements, so too have politicians. As *CrimethInc.* recently argued, Trump's electoral win does not signal the coming of fascism, but instead white supremacy attempting to rearticulate itself:

> "*Fascism is not just any extreme right-wing position. It is a complex phenomenon that mobilizes a popular movement under the hierarchical direction of a political party and cultivates parallel loyalty structures in the police and military, to conquer power either through democratic or military means; subsequently abolishes electoral procedures to guarantee a single party continuity; creates a new social contract with the domestic working class, on the one hand ushering in a higher standard of living than what could be achieved under liberal capitalism and on the other hand protecting the capitalists with a new social peace; and eliminates the internal enemies whom it had blamed for the destabilization of the prior regime.*

> "*Trump showed contempt for democratic convention by threatening to intimidate voters and hinting that he might not concede a lost election, but his model of conservatism in no way abolishes the mechanisms that are fundamental to democracy.*

> "*There is, in fact, nothing fascist about Trump.*"

They go on to write:

> "*Although the billionaire's narrative of victimization— which the media has compliantly disseminated—is frankly pathetic, whiteness in the United States is*

indeed facing a crisis. Not because 'whites are becoming a minority' or any other paranoid supremacist fantasy, but because in the last few decades, the paramilitary functions of whiteness have largely been absorbed by an increasingly powerful government that can do with judges, prisons, and urban redevelopment bureaucracies what yesteryear it had to do with lynch mobs—to such an extent that, paradoxically, even a black man can be put in charge of the whole apparatus.

"Before Trump, the Tea Party movement began speaking to the crisis of whiteness, and was rewarded with an outpouring of support. The Donald simply named the anxiety more explicitly, and spoke from a larger platform.

"Whiteness was created to destroy solidarity among the oppressed and to encourage loyalty to the rulers. On the streets of Ferguson and other cities, we saw how it also completes the paramilitary function of disarming people of color and preventing white people from directly taking part in the rebellions where racial divisions start to finally melt down.

"Whiteness is a war measure. There are a thousand forms of mutiny, but all of them require the recognition that a war is going on."

But to get to the heart of their thesis:

"The media in general have suggested that Trump's appeals to whites were so effective because of the economic situation: working-class whites have felt threatened as their privileges and their social standing decline, so the story goes. Yet the racial gaps in wealth and standard of living have grown since the crisis. If economics were the bottom line, white Americans would feel more secure, not less secure, after Obama's presidency. White

> *privilege, in this sense, continues to pay its dividends. I*
> *would argue that it is actually the paramilitary func-*
> *tion that is an ingrained part of whiteness which is in*
> *crisis, and which mobilized large numbers of whites for*
> *Trump."*[7]

In short, the material and psychological wage of the cross-class white supremacist compact is still being paid out to white workers, but actions that used to be carried out by self-organized paramilitary organizations are now instead handled by a massive, bureaucratic, and neoliberal state.

Trump, just like the alt-right, saw a potential base within this reality, and acted accordingly. In many ways, this mirrors previous election cycles such as those of Barry Goldwater and George Wallace. Both campaigns saw massive support from various white supremacist groups, from the KKK to neonazis. In the case of Wallace, out of the ashes of his campaign's failure came one organization, the National Youth Alliance for Wallace, which spawned the National Alliance, whose leader William Pierce would go on to publish the *Turner Diaries*, inspiring a wide range of terrorist groups from The Order to Timothy McVeigh.

Back in our current period, the response to Trump's electoral victory from white nationalists, including and in particular the alt-right, has been extremely lackluster. We mean this in the sense that the majority of the movement seems to be giving Trump the benefit of the doubt, concentrating on "holding his feet to the fire" in the hopes of influencing the regime. Groups such as the Traditionalist Worker Party have articulated such a standpoint at the risk of alienating some of their supporters. As one angry commenter wrote on their website:

---

7. CrimethInc., "Trump: Fascism or White Supremacy?" *It's Going Down* (online), December 13, 2016.

"So another WN group falls to the wayside through
Trump worship. He was only worth supporting because
he disparaged all the other candidates in a corrupt
system. But he always was a crony capitalist piece of shit,
and now he should be treated as such accordingly.

"You should be working to bring down the system like
the radical left does. Instead, you idolize someone who
has been in bed with jew finance his entire life. America
went into serfdom with the Trump supported bank bail-
outs of 2008. He granted them permanent rent seeking
status when he did that, and it was pure treason."

On the alt-right, those in the leadership of "the movement" are
pushing to influence the Trump regime in extremely organized
ways. For instance, Richard Spencer is moving the National
Policy Institute to Washington DC to be closer to the administration. According to *Forward.com*, "Richard Spencer now lists
Arlington Virginia as NPI's headquarters and says he plans to
spend more time in Washington DC as the 'alt-right' continues
its efforts to influence the mainstream."[8]

Identity Evropa has articulated that the alt-right needs to
push harder to take over the mainstream of the right-wing in
the wake of Trump. Speaking on the recent NPI conference
they wrote:

"There was a will to capitalize as fully as possible on
Trump's win. At the conference, you got a real sense of
where this movement is going. That we are the intellectual vanguard of the American right cannot be doubted.
Now is the time to press harder than we have before
to make ourselves and our ideas more prominent on
the national stage. Our movement is no longer a head

---

8. Sam Kestenbaum, "In Montana, Activists and a Rabbi Resist the Resident
White Supremacist." *Forward* (online), December 15, 2016.

*without a body. We have the momentum to propel
ourselves into the future, and Identity Evropa will be on
the front lines of this fight helping to lead our people to a
better and brighter future."*[9]

To date, there has been repeated crossover between the Trump campaign and the alt-right, such as the connections made with *Breitbart* and its chief editor Steve Bannon who is now appointed to Trump's cabinet, Donald Trump, Jr. coming on the white nationalist podcast *The Political Cesspool*, neonazis and white nationalists staffing Trump offices, various white power groups doing calls and volunteering for Trump, to many within the Trump campaign following white nationalists on Twitter and Trump parroting much of Alex Jones's talking points, to Trump even outright retweeting memes from white supremacist Twitter accounts. While this is certainly enough to make one sick, on the other hand the regime has been quick to distance themselves from much of the far right, Eric Trump even going so far as to say that David Duke "deserves a bullet."

What is more clear is that the Trump campaign mined the alt-right for talking points, soundbites, and ideas. While those on the alt-right would be overjoyed for this relationship to continue and deepen, on top of putting more and more of their people inside the establishment, it seems unlikely that the current regime is going to be enough to satisfy the white nationalist movement over an extended period of time.

It is also worth noting that the move made by the NPI to land in DC in order to influence politics as usual, echoes very much the Liberty Lobby headed by Willis Carto, which functioned in much the same way from 1958 until 2001. With an office in downtown DC, the Liberty Lobby presented itself much as the current alt-right does; as the defenders of "true" conservatism and with no ties to outright antisemitism or

9. Karl North, "NPI 2016," *Identity Evropa* (online) November 29, 2016.

neonazism. While the politics of the organization were clear to many, Carto was also quick to set up many other side organizations, such as the Institute for Historical Review (which was based around Hitler worship, studying the third reich, and Holocaust Denial), as well as *The Spotlight* publication, which reported white nationalist news on everything from Patrick Buchanan to neonazi skinheads.

But the Liberty Lobby was also a lesson in the tendency of far right groups to splinter and fracture. Carto established the National Youth Alliance for George Wallace, only to lose it to William Pierce. He helped establish the Populist Party, only to watch as wave after wave of participants dropped out once the group's ties to Nazis and the Klan came more out into the open. Fights, often violent and leading to drawn out court cases, broke out between various factions over mailing lists, which at the time were the lifeblood of such organizations staying afloat, because they meant access to donations.

In the end, the Liberty Lobby placed its bet on politics and the electoral runs of Patrick Buchanan, only to see them fail time after time. Eventually the Liberty Lobby fell apart after lawsuits and splits. Carto was buried in a cemetery for Veterans. Before he died he joked, "I'm probably America's biggest Hitler fan, but I'll be buried alongside all these World War II vets ..."

All in all, we don't see things playing out much differently for the alt-right in today's current environment, but we have a role to play in their downfall as well.

THE ALT-RIGHT AND THE MEDIA, THE MEDIA AND US

Revolutionary anarchists and anti-fascists will never be given the same spotlight as the alt-right is getting, we need to accept this reality and deal with it.

The alt-right is an abnormality to the media, one that it

finds enticing because it is a white supremacist movement that doesn't *look like one*. This is a story that they will never get tired of telling, and as white nationalists are America's number one killers, it's unlikely to stop grabbing headlines anytime soon. But in doing so, they will normalize and spread the basic talking points of the alt-right far and wide. And, as the Trump campaign has shown, many of these formerly extreme positions are becoming much more center of the road.

The media loves the alt-right because it plays by the rules. The alt-right doesn't organize massive shut downs, occupations, strikes, and riots like we do—first of all, they can't, but moreover, they fill out paperwork for permits and work with the police. The alt-right doesn't bloc up and cover their faces with ski masks in order to avoid arrest, they hide behind the police and look for media people to tell their side of the story to. The alt-right is an upper middle class package of "activism" that already makes sense to the media: legalistic, seemingly following the rules, clean-cut, articulate, male, and of course: *totally white*. Finally a social movement that was made for air time!

To beat our head against a wall and continue to point out that far right white men have killed more police officers than anyone and that white nationalists make up the biggest terrorist threat on American soil, is a losing struggle in the face of the media. The media isn't interested in the truth, *they're interested in selling papers and advertising*.

The mainstream media will never paint us in a similar positive light, nor allow us to articulate our ideas; our movement will always be anathema to them. Revolutionary anarchism and militant anti-fascism flies in the face of everything that the mainstream bourgeois media holds dear. We don't want basic reforms to the system, we want a social revolution that changes life fundamentally on all levels. We don't work legalistically to hold polite demonstrations; when possible, we shut down streets, attack the storefronts of corporations, clash with police, occupy buildings, and go out on strike. Also, unlike the alt-right, our movement is multi-racial and involves people of various backgrounds, genders, and sexualities. To paraphrase something Noam Chomsky once said, if the media was smarter it would allow radicals on the air more often, in order to make them look completely alien. For the media, it is clear which side is more "camera ready."

While we do not think we should shy away from stating our positions to the mainstream media when given the opportunity, we think the continued belief held by many Leftists that more media will bring us closer to our goals is a mistake. While popularizing and normalizing our ideas is important to all of us, ultimately we will have to do this through our own infrastructure and networks. Furthermore, if anarchist ideas are to have any sort of currency, they will have to be backed up with action and people's ability to become involved in organizing, fighting, and building a different way of life—not just sharing memes, Twitter updates, and listening to podcasts.

As always, we need to think about how we can use our online resources to grow the existing movement we have on the streets, not retreat farther and farther back into cyberspace.

THE ALT-RIGHT ISN'T ALL RIGHT

As we have laid out in this essay, there are major challenges facing the alt-right, and the far right more broadly, that will continue to play out, especially as Trump is now the head of a new regime. We see these as:

▶ Questions of class: Many in white nationalist circles have long laughed at the alt-right as an upper middle class movement, and we see this trend continuing. As the alt-right tries to transition into street action, more and more they will also come up against their upper middle class base being a problem. Moreover, the reality that anti-fascists are willing to physically confront them means that they will have to consider how they will respond. While we hold no illusions that groups such as Identity Evropa would beat the shit out of us if they could or were able, at the same time, we know that currently their image would be tarnished if they were portrayed on the same footing as anti-fascists, fighting in the streets. While the media may love their "dapper" rich boys now, once violence enters into the equation they will be quick to turn them into "menacing supremacist thugs." But *if* the far right is to grow beyond the confines of the internet, it *will* need bodies in the street to protect the leadership of its elitist cadre. Thus, at some point the alt-right will most likely attempt to make common cause with the more "traditional" white power movement in order to provide muscle (as Matthew Heimbach has done) or will simply attempt to openly recruit from the white working class and the poor. While the idea of Richard Spencer trying to recruit poor whites is laughable, the question of class will continue to dog the alt-right.

▶ Questions of violence: As Nathan Damigo wrote recently on Twitter, the failure of the current "work within the system" breed of alt-right organizers will lead to a much more violent collection of white nationalist militants. While of course in the US and around the world we've seen the growth of far right violence and terrorism for decades, it is very possible that this tendency will grow and expand as it is felt by the broad base of the insurgent far right that Trump (and overall democracy) has failed them. As this shift happens, questions of violence will again take center stage and the movement will continue to fracture over disagreements.

▶ Questions of tactics: Many on the far right proclaimed that Trump was their last electoral hope. That if Trump lost, the only possible way to uphold white supremacy in the United States would be to create a revolutionary movement that took state power. While it appears that many on the far right and the alt-right are biding their time and waiting for the Trump Train to roll out, eventually Trump will begin to disappoint them just like any other politician. At that point, perhaps several years down the line, the movement will split again over questions of what to do. Should they again put all their chips behind a candidate? Or instead focus more on building a movement? Only time will tell who will go where, but in the end, not everyone will be on the same page.

▶ Question on links to neonazism: As the reaction to "HeilGate" shows, not everyone in white nationalism is on the same page, and moreover many are quick to sell out their former comrades if they feel the heat is too hot. While overall, white nationalists are attempting to move into a more "mainstream" appearance (getting rid of swastikas, etc.), as was stated before, this is still a subculture that was built on memes with Hitler in them and references to "14/88." One thing is clear, that publically, many on the alt-right, and even amongst white nationalists, want to avoid being labeled neonazis or white supremacists. Anti-fascists can continue to expose the connections between these groups while also explaining how their ideas are essentially the same, despite the various degrees of separation or aesthetic differences that they have.

LESSONS AND CHALLENGES

In closing, revolutionary anarchists and anti-fascists have several lessons to take away from the current moment:

▶ The mainstream media is not our friend and currently is in a crisis and losing money. While it presents itself as a neutral force within society and as a watchdog against wrongdoing, in reality it is designed to sell advertising and is driven by the same forces that own it. While the media acts as "shocked and appalled" by the growth of the alt-right, it at the same time does not understand how to be against a fascist movement that does not look how they expect a fascist movement to look and on the surface, appears to be legalistic and democratic in nature. While we expect the hype around the alt-right will fade with time, we cannot expect the same kind of spotlight on our movements due to the aims that we hold and our revolutionary ideas and militant actions. We must deal with the normalization of far right ideas by continuing to promote and popularize our own.

▶ The alt-right and the much larger insurgent far right have grown in size in the wake of black insurgency and the growth of popular social movements and struggles from below, not simply as a consequence of the Trump campaign. Like Trump, however, the alt-right is seeking to harness this reaction into support for political power, albeit in a completely different fashion.

▶ The alt-right will splinter and fracture under the Trump regime. Some will fall away. Others will toe the classic line of "hold our elected leaders accountable," while others will call for militant action. In time, many will attempt to break with legalistic and democratic tactics, while others will argue against such measures. Overall, the alt-right will also have to come to terms with the fact that it is an *elitist* movement that does not have much of a rank and file that can operate in the streets. Instead, the alt-right seems more interested in working *inside* the system, rather than against it. Eventually, these positions will lead to more and more splits, and the Trump era of unity will again be shattered.

In closing, we face several challenges:

▶ How do we confront a fascist force that does not operate on ground that we are used to, or even have access to? What do you do about a group of people who are members of a frat which had five presidents come through its doors?[10] How do we combat white nationalists who are corporate lawyers and have vast amounts of family money at their disposal? If we know anything (or think we know) about political people in positions of wealth and power it's this: *they don't like to be embarrassed.* Let's drag their names and their politics through the mud, as much as possible. At their homes, at their work, at their school, everywhere. Let's remind everyone that we offer no platform and no peace for fascists. As the May 1st Anarchist Alliance wrote recently on their analysis of a disruption of a Milo event:

> *"One of the middle class students waiting for Milo made a racist remark, and I said he was a middle class piece of shit. He corrected me and said he was upper middle class. He was afraid of being included with the regular middle class and no doubt horrified at the thought of being identified with the working classes, but where is he going? Somehow I assume he sees his future as being tied with gaining/maintaining the upper hand against working people, communities of color, women, Muslims,*

---

10. "Michigan Identity Evropa: Fraternity of Fascists." Northern California Anti-Racist Action (NoCARA) (online), December 12, 2016.

Latinos, and so on. He hopes that by allying himself with
Milo and Trump and a developing fascist movement, he
will carve out a space for himself and comfort for himself
at the expense of people beneath him. He wants to join
with Milo and Trump to be on top against the rest of us.

"The cops escorted Milo into the hall through another
entrance and then attacked the anti-fascist forces and
opened the way for Milo's supporters to enter the hall.
This frenzy of trying to gain advantage at someone else's
expense, this frenzy of hating women and Muslims, this
frenzy of taking up white nationalism and war fever,
these are the dangers. This is not the old time klan, these
college students are so lame that they think it makes
them hip to support Milo and to embrace or consider
embracing fascism."[11]

▶ We have to build up a presence on college campuses again
and not leave the schools to become playgrounds for the
far right. Let's work to build connections on campus, both
with groups when possible, and networks of friends.

▶ Continue organizing militant confrontations with fascists,
keep releasing their info, and stay up on counter-recruiting.
Give them no quarter, go after them in every way, and build
up a capacity to out-organize them.

▶ Confront their ideas politically. We have to attack the foun-
dational ideas of white nationalism head on within wider
society. We have to expose and show how concepts that
seek to justify fascism and an authoritarian system are false
and work against poor and working people. This requires
us talking and organizing with people as much as it requires

---

11. B.D., "Fighting the Alt-Right: Report and Analysis of Michigan State
University protest." First of May Anarchist Alliance (online), December 15, 2016.

our showing that there are different ways of thinking critically about society beyond false and racist notions that "the Jews run the world."

Our movement has survived everything from Pinkertons, the KKK, Russian gulags, to World Wars. One thing is clear, *we ain't afraid of no memes.*

Black Genocide
and the Alt-Right

K. Kersplebedeb

Discussions about the Alternative Right normally mention the movement's white nationalism, its connections to white supremacist organizations historically and at present, and its social base of young alienated white men. It is well known that the movement is made up of racists, and indeed its flagship organization, the National Policy Institute, was founded in 2005 (prior to the alt-right's rise), precisely to promote white theories of supposed black inferiority, and "to elevate the consciousness of whites, ensure our biological and cultural continuity, and protect our civil rights."[1]

That said, alt-right views about black people are often not explored in detail. Two possible reasons for this present themselves; to provide an accurate picture of alt-right race politics and what they imply, it is important that these be stated explicitly.

First, tragically but simply enough, the history and present reality of US racism is such that the alt-right, like the rest of the far right, does not always stand out as being all that extreme. Whereas their support for dictatorship, dreams of dismembering America, and their hostility to Jews and women might be repulsive to most white people and place them on the political

---

1. Devin Burghart, "Who is Richard Spencer?" *Institute For Research & Education On Human Rights,* June 27, 2014.

fringe, their anti-black views are often just a less polite articulation of what significant numbers of white Americans consider to be an acceptable opinion.

As such, when discussing black people, the alt-right focus is often on attacking groups defending black human rights, while exculpating whites for, or explaining away, the conditions in which black people already find themselves. These are fairly common white positions, even amongst "liberals"; for a white movement to hold such views is hardly news. Even their goal of a white "ethnostate" is not so incongruous: legislation and extralegal violence excluding people from a jurisdiction on the basis of "race" are a mainstay of American history. Indeed, a major alt-right talking-point, that the United States was historically meant to be a country for white men, is just a truth that cannot be denied.

In other words, the white supremacism of the alt-right is compatible with regular racist US "democracy"; an example of what J. Sakai once observed, that in North America, "settlerism filled the space that fascism normally occupies."[2]

A second possible reason why alt-right anti-black racism garners less attention than their views on queer people, Jews, or women, is that the latter are somewhat contested and in some ways open to change, while regarding black people, there is just the same old dreary white supremacist consistency. There are no debates in alt-right circles about including black people in their movement, or complicated theories about black conspiracies controlling the world. Instead, articles on alt-right websites mock blacks murdered by police as "dindu nuffins," promote pseudo-scientific theories about a genetic tendency to low intelligence and high criminality, and routinely smear Black Lives Matter and similar groups as racist, terrorist, "thugs." Indeed, as this book was being prepared for press,

---

2. J. Sakai, *When Race Burns Class: Settlers Revisited*, (Montreal: Kersplebedeb, 2011), 20. Also available online at the *Kersplebedeb* website.

alt-rightists succeeded in leveraging their internet presence to reframe the torture of a mentally disabled white teenager in Chicago as an anti-white hate crime carried out by Black Lives Matter, this despite the fact that there was zero indication of any connection whatsoever between the group and the assailants in question.[3]

Often, alt-rightists present matters in terms of white victimhood, framing their politics as a matter of self-defense. On the American Renaissance website, Hubert Collins recounts his own adolescence and how it shaped his current politics:

> [T]he schools were trying to turn our minds against the evidence of our senses. They tried to inculcate the conviction that all groups are equal in every way. I knew that wasn't true. Blacks were menacing. They were dangerous. My understanding of white identity came from the desire for safety, and the realization that safety meant the company of people like me. [...] for those of us raised in the multiracial cesspools that will soon spread to the whole country, the question of identity always boils down to the question of safety. To me, it is safety that makes white identity so important, so meaningful, and so long lasting.[4]

Proceeding on the basis of such "white safety," others put a further gloss on their message, painting a picture of an all-white nirvana that means no one any harm. Theodore Beale would have us believe that alt-right just means that "everyone should be left by they own damn selves,"[5] while Brad Griffin tells us how Jews will all be happy in Israel and blacks in Africa, if they

---

3. Bryan Menegus, "Alt-Right Trolls Use Chicago Kidnapping to Spread Lies About Black Lives Matter." *Gizmodo* (online), January 5, 2017.

4. Hubert Collins, "Why I'm a Race Realist." *American Renaissance* (online), August 12, 2015

5. Vox Day, "Alt-Right: What It Is." *Vox Popoli* (online), November 24, 2014.

only leave whites to "their" America.[6] Yet despite this cheerful talk of "separate but equal" ethnostates, the alt-right's underlying fear of black people invariably leads in a more historically predictable direction. As George Ciccariello-Maher (himself a target of an alt-right internet doxxing and hate campaign) recently put it, "What is important to remember about white fragility and white discomfort is that when white people are scared, people die."[7] So it comes as no surprise to find one article in *The Right Stuff* calling for (in preventive self-defense, of course!) "the largest genocide the world has seen" against the "dindu nations,"[8] while Lawrence Murray opines that for America to deal with "a people who cannot achieve parity," "we essentially need some form of fascism,"[9] whereas Robert Finstock considers "a continent-wide sterilization campaign in Africa."[10] There is really no difference between the alt-right's dreams and the murderous reality of a Dylann Roof—as Roof put it to his victims just before he opened fire, "I have to do it. You rape our women and you're taking over our country. And you have to go."

---

6. Hunter Wallace, "White-Collar Supremacy," *Occidental Dissent* (online), November 25, 2016. One assumes such visions of what Richard Spencer once termed "peaceful ethnic cleansing" are not only tongue-and-cheek, but also reflect a real sense amongst such racists that their programme doesn't *need* to be violent (if only everyone else would just cooperate!). While this is not the place to refute such white dreams, it is worth noting how much they rely on normalizing settlerism and leaving Indigenous people out of the equation. Taking everyone into account reveals how even in its most sanitized versions, the ethnostate model always implies displacement, oppression, and genocide.

7. Quoted in Monique Judge, "White Fragility Leads to White Violence: Why Conversations About Race With White People Fall Apart." *The Root* (online), January 15, 2017.

8. Prez Jeff Davis, "Genocide: The Inescapable Conclusion." *The Right Stuff* (online), December 5, 2016.

9. Lawrence Murray, "Antebellum Dindu Adventure: The Birth of a Nation." *Atlantic Centurion* (online), October 10, 2016.

10. Robert Finstock, "A Northern Alliance: Our Ultimate Salvation." *Counter-Currents Publishing* (online), January 2017.

That the alt-right's programme is implicitly genocidal is not to say that details don't matter. In terms of understanding the movement's appeal and possibilities for growth, as well as the subjective reality of its members, their defensive posture and "positive" utopianism are a different shade of white from either traditional Nazis or Jim Crow-era Kluxers. In a sense, their ideology is a kind of post-nazism, bearing the mark of the neo-colonial age in which it was born.

Nonetheless, the new jar holds the same sour wine: when "white nationalism," "race realism," "ethnostate," and similar terms are used, dispossession and murder are always being implied. There is no such thing as "white racial purity" or "white nationalism" without anti-black racism and genocide.

Notes on Trump

Bromma

1. THE NORMALITY OF WHITE SUPREMACY

Since Trump's election, I keep hearing that we shouldn't "normalize" him or his agenda. I believe that's looking through the wrong end of the telescope. There's nothing as "normal" in the US as white supremacy. Sometimes it's disguised by tokenism and obscured by "multiculturalism." But in this country, white supremacy has always shown its true naked face at times of stress and transition.

Because white supremacy isn't just a bunch of bad ideas inherited from ignorant elders. It's a deeply-rooted institution through which the US rules over many oppressed peoples. It's the glue that keeps hundred of millions loyal to that very same program. It's the central ideological, political, and physical system set up by white capital to rule the land and dominate its internal and external colonies. And therefore, white supremacy underpins all the wealth and power this country's ruling class possesses. Without it, the US falls.

2. CONTRADICTIONS WITHIN WHITE CAPITALISM

White supremacy is constant, but it keeps changing form. For instance, African Americans have endured a variety of modes of white supremacy: slavery, Jim Crow, gentrification, and more. White capitalism welcomed Mexicans and Chinese as semi-slave laborers, then attacked and deported them when conditions changed. Native peoples faced extermination campaigns, phony treaties, forced assimilation, and confinement on reservations, depending on what mode of genocide seemed most effective for settler society at various times. White supremacy isn't a single, one-dimensional attack by white society on people of color. The form can change, as long as whiteness is always valued; as long as white people are always on top.

US white supremacy was modified in response to world anti-colonial struggles and, after the Cold War, to globalization. Together these developments generated significant contradictions for traditional forms of white supremacy.

By the late 1970s, the US's old-style white military colonialism had lost much of its power, beaten back by a phalanx of national liberation struggles. Out of necessity, US imperialism rebooted, searching out non-white colonial partners and adopting new forms of "colorblind" financial blackmail to replace or supplement white military occupation. In this new political landscape, overt chauvinism was often counterproductive; it created friction for the imperial agenda.

In the 1990s, the world economy entered a period of particularly intense capitalist globalization. Economic borders became weaker, protectionist barriers to trade and investment fell, and monopoly capitalists everywhere embraced the transnational integration of markets and finance. US capitalists profited massively from this wave of globalization. Some of the biggest US-based corporations began to see themselves as global businesses, floating above national markets and politics. They eagerly sought out non-white overseas partners to initiate cross-border industries, investments and supply lines. They promoted multilateral trade deals with far-flung overseas allies. They sat side by side with Asians and Latin Americans on boards of directors, and decided major economic policies in integrated international forums. They debated how to create global political institutions to go along with a global economy. A whole stratum of corporate leaders, and their children, saw themselves as part of a transcultural elite. Open, blatant racism wasn't helpful in this changing environment.

Gradually, the US ruling class adapted white supremacy to these new conditions and gave it a new look. In the revised, neocolonial order, some people of color were coopted into positions of wealth and authority. Racist violence and discrimination continued inside and outside the country. But at the same time, especially as globalization surged, US high culture increasingly professed to celebrate the diversity of all nationalities and races (and genders too). This helped present US imperialism to its colonies, its multinational business partners, and to the rest of the world, with a friendlier face. White supremacy continued, altered in form by neocolonialism and disguised by capitalist multiculturalism.

3. MULTICULTURALISM CHALLENGED

Some white people embraced the concept of multiculturalism, sincerely hoping it could be the basis for a genuine progressive culture. But most white amerikans felt that this new incarnation of capitalism was a demotion. They didn't like having people of color as their bosses. They didn't like seeing "good jobs" and social bribery spread around the world, instead of being reserved for them. And they hated the "political correctness" of having to hide their racism. US capitalism's perceived "disloyalty" to its white home base during the rise of globalization fueled the current upsurge of right-wing populism, including eventually the campaign of Donald Trump.

But for quite a while the ruling class turned a deaf ear to its disgruntled white masses. The capitalists had global interests to tend to; global profits to bank. To be blunt, a willing Asian dictator or Latina judge or African American president was worth more to them than a thousand whining white people. The militia movement was repressed when it became too militant; the Tea Party was mocked by the global sophisticates. (Neither was destroyed, though; they each remained as a possibility, a fallback.)

As globalization continued to advance in the last few decades, white amerika was gradually forced and cajoled to accept modest changes in the hierarchy of imperial privilege. It seemed possible that monopoly capital, pushing white people to fall in line with multiculturalism, might continue forever along that path, backed and cheered by cohorts of optimistic and idealistic artists and intellectuals.

To a large extent, this is where the plaintive cry not to "normalize" Trump comes from. Cosmopolitan liberals, now accustomed to living under globalized capitalism, simply can't believe that US society will be allowed to go backward; can't believe that a rich country could ever be permitted to trash multiculturalism; to turn back the clock on women's rights and environmentalism and so much more. They have a hard time accepting that their bright dream of a blended world culture, a dream that had previously been tolerated and even encouraged by major sectors of monopoly capital, might be betrayed, and end in a surge of old-fashioned racist violence. Their disbelief echoes the disbelief among the liberal intelligentsia in England after Brexit, and in other countries where globalization is giving ground.

4. TIMING IS EVERYTHING

It's important to understand that populist opposition to globalization in the West is making breakthroughs not as globalization rises, but as it falters. In fact, the rise of these political movements is probably more a *reflection* of globalization's decline than the *cause* of that decline. What's coming into view, semi-hidden underneath the frenzied soap opera of reactionary populism, is that the tide of globalization has crested and started to recede. It wasn't permanent after all.

It should be stipulated, right off the bat, that globalization has unleashed immense changes, many of which are irreversible. For example, the peasantry, once the largest class of all, isn't coming back. Globalization broke it; sent it streaming out of the countryside by the hundreds of millions. Out of that broken peasantry, a giant new woman-centered proletariat and a sprawling lumpen-proletariat are still being formed around the world.

Yet globalization as a financially-integrated, transnational form of capitalism can't advance without constant expansion, without constant profit growth. Since no global state exists to mediate among the world's capitalists, shared growth is the only thing that restrains them from cut-throat competition. Growth is also what allows capitalists to at least partly mollify the displaced masses back home with cheap commodities and whatever jobs a rising world economy has to offer. But now, instead of growing, the world economy is slowing. In fact, globalized capitalism, having bulked up on steroidal injections of speculation and unsustainable leveraged debt, is teetering on the edge of disaster.

From the US to China, from the Eurozone to Brazil, danger signs are flashing; massive globalized industries are shifting into reverse. International trade and investment are flat or falling. Capital that was formerly used for investment in "emerging economies" is now flowing backward into safe haven investments in the metropolis. Automation, renewable energy and other new technologies are starting to shorten supply chains, reducing the demand for imports from far away. Intractable economic and political crises, like those in the Middle East and Greece and Ukraine, are eroding cooperation and sapping confidence in already-weak globalist institutions. The internet, a key factor in globalization, is gradually becoming segmented, as governments and corporations privatize, censor, and manipulate parts of it. Migration is slowing. And underneath everything, the increased inequality caused by globalization itself is throttling the demand for commodities.

Multinational corporations aren't abandoning world markets by any means. But leading monopoly capitalists are hedging their bets; reducing their reliance on complex, interdependent trade and finance. Facing what he calls a "protectionist global environment," GE CEO Jeffrey Immelt is shifting his company's production from a globalized to a "localized" model. "We used to have one site to make locomotives; now we have multiple global sites that give us market access. A localization strategy can't be shut down by protectionist policies." This is a defensive posture, anticipating a less globalized form of imperialism. Transnational supply lines, labor forces, and markets are the most profitable as long as globalization rules. But they are vulnerable to political disruption when globalization retreats.

Looking at recent history, one big indication of globalization's exhaustion is its inability to "digest" Central Asia or the Middle East, blocked by armed struggle movements of Islamist fundamentalists. This failure comes as a shock to capitalists, shaking their confidence. It also emboldens opponents of globalization in the West. In a sense the Trump and Brexit movements are pale and privileged echoes of vanguard right-wing populists in the colonial world—reactionary rebels who demonstated globalization's limitations with their bodies and weapons.

Once it appeared that global capitalist integration had unstoppable momentum. But now a retreat into the once-familiar zones of old-fashioned nation-based imperialism seems to be on the capitalist menu.

5. A PREVIOUS WAVE OF GLOBALIZATION

If the ongoing shift away from transnationalism and towards harsh national rivalry continues, it won't be the first instance of "de-globalization" in modern history. It's happened before.

From 1870 to 1913, fueled by the industrial revolution and

the explosive rise of US capitalism, there was a massive spike in international trade and market integration. It was centered in Western Europe and the US, but extended into Latin America and other parts of the world, too. Borders were opened, tariffs were lowered, and there was a rapid increase in cross-border investment and multinational financial cooperation. The world capitalist economy boomed. Just as during the current wave of globalization, this earlier period was marked by major innovations in transport and communications, as well as an unprecedented upsurge in transnational migration. (Including tens of millions of workers who migrated from Europe to the US.) Economists refer to this as the "first wave" of modern globalization.

But capitalism is at best an unstable and contradictory system, periodically riven by economic crisis. And a globalized form of capitalism, with its web of interdependencies, appears to be particularly vulnerable to those crises.

The globalization of 1870–1913 collapsed like a house of cards. Growing economic imbalances and stalled growth led many imperialist countries to impose tariffs and other protectionist measures, vainly striving to boost their own home economy at the expense of others. Inevitably, there was retaliation in kind. This cannibalistic inter-imperial competition only aggravated the already deteriorating economic conditions. Trade and global commodities became more and more expensive. There was a rapid downward spiral of economic depression and reactionary nationalism.

There was no pretense of multiculturalism in the US back then, of course. Massive violence against people of color was already common during the boom years of globalization. So it's hard to say if racism became worse in this country during the period of de-globalization. But in 1913, segregation was officially initiated in all federal offices, lunchrooms, and bathrooms. In the following decades there were dozens of vicious race riots against Black enclaves in cities North and South, causing many hundreds of deaths and thousands of people driven from their homes. Having been pushed down previously, the Klan was revived in 1915. Its peak was in the 1920s, with some 4 million members. In the 1930s, as the world economic crisis deepened, millions of Mexicans and Mexican Americans were deported.

The first wave of globalization imploded in a frenzy of national hatred and two brutal world wars, fought without quarter among the capitalist powers. Something we should keep in mind as we confront the current situation.

6. DE-GLOBALIZATION

Today's capitalist globalization isn't failing because of political blows landed by Western anti-globalization movements, although those have had a real effect. Rather, the populist movements are reaching for real power just as factions of the ruling class globalist consensus are themselves breaking away and seeking alternate, nationalistic strategies.

Former globalizers are floating back toward the anchors of their old home economies and shifting the blame for economic crisis onto "foreigners" and social minorities. They're muting their former advocacy of free trade while backing away from trade agreements. They're rediscovering protectionism. They're experimenting with cyber-attacks on other countries, building up their militaries, increasing their involvement in proxy wars, and manipulating their currencies to gain temporary advantage over trading partners. And as a natural part of this shift, they're unleashing their most rabid "patriotic" social bases to sell their new/old program, control the streets, and set themselves up as potential cannon fodder down the road.

In every quarter of the globe, nationalistic xenophobia is on the rise, strangling the remaining globalists' fading dreams about world government and a borderless economy. Right-wing populism is being released, and it's rising out of its reservoirs, flowing like water filling dry river beds. In country after country, old social prejudices are being revived and intensified; former globalist capitalists are reaching out and mending fences with their most trusted national social bases.

That's how it is here in the US, too. A return to the old white amerika is becoming a more and more practical program for US capitalists—not just for the white masses. It offers the only "natural" form of capitalist regroupment in this country as globalization wanes. An option as amerikan as apple pie.

Neo-colonialism isn't going away—it's become a deep strategic necessity for modern imperialism. But mass multiculturalism is just a tactic for the capitalists, subject to revision or reversal. A wiser comrade once warned me, during the rise of globalization, that the ruling class would someday "give amerika back to white people." That's what seems to be happening with Trump. (Whether or not the capitalists can control the populists they are unleashing remains, as always, an open question.)

7. CAPITALISTS SHIFT GEARS

The recent wave of accelerated globalization that started in the 1990s was led by a bloc of Western capital, along with Japan and other close allies in Asia. There were two key geopolitical factors in its take-off. One was the formation of the EU, which consolidated European capital, including parts of the old Soviet empire. The EU also provided a model for what a globalized borderless world might look like, complete with transnational institutions and regulations.

The second factor was a tacit agreement between Western capital and China to collaborate on capitalist development. China supplied a low-wage labor force to produce cheap commodities, enabling enormous profits for investors. In return, the Chinese state and Party skimmed off some of those profits, retained significant control over investment decisions, built modern infrastructure and accumulated advanced technology.

This "win-win" capitalist model, involving high-level financial integration and lowered trade barriers, was eventually expanded to other countries.

Both of these key factors of globalization appear to be disintegrating. When times were good in Europe, national jealousies were kept in check. But with the economic slowdown, and now with the refugee crisis originating in the Middle East, centrifugal forces are rising inside the EU. Brexit is only one example. As for the deal with China, that was always a marriage of convenience. The West never planned to let China become a serious imperial rival. While on the other hand, Chinese capitalists planned from the very beginning to use globalization as a springboard to empire.

Globalization has always encountered some opposition among capitalists. In many cases, that opposition comes from businesspeople based in a single country, who resent having to compete with the flood of cheap imports from abroad. It also comes from the more rabid proponents of national imperial power. They think military force and economic blackmail can be more profitable than friendly internationalism. When globalization starts to show weakness, these opponents see opportunity, and fight hard to shift the capitalist consensus.

For some time, a group of Republican lawmakers have been chomping at the bit to take China and Russia down a notch. They've fumed as foreign capital bought up businesses and property in the US, and issued dire warnings that imperial rivals were supplanting the US in Asia, Africa, Latin America, and the Middle East. In a parallel political universe, a group of Democrats, egged on by the unions, demanded more tariffs, "local sourcing" regulations, and other protections from "free trade."

Each of these forces represented a piece of the anti-globalist agenda. Each was in the minority. Neither cared for Trump because he was an outsider and a loose cannon. But Trump finds himself in a position to put the pieces together.

There was significant ruling class support for Trump's campaign from the beginning—including Kenneth Langone of Home Depot, Peter Thiel of PayPal, David Green of Hobby Lobby, and plenty more. Now Republican politicians, manufacturers, tech billionaires, oil company executives, and Goldman Sachs bankers are lining up to apply for cabinet jobs and making pilgrimages to Trump Tower to "consult" with the anti-globalizer-in-chief.

Although most British capitalists initially opposed the Brexit campaign, many also backed it. The supporters saw it as an opportunity to "deregulate" and privatize the economy and to make trade deals specifically favoring England. In China, a country that was once the poster child for globalization, the ruling class has made the conscious decision to become less dependent on exports to the West. They want to build up their home market. Moreover, they are responding to a weakening economy by fomenting xenophobia and populist narratives of imperial glory to come. In Russia, patriotic fervor and expansionist dreams are the only thing keeping Putin's corrupt authoritarian regime afloat. This trend of rising capitalist antiglobalization is general, worldwide.

As the US starts to hunker down—starts to game-out possible trade wars and military conflicts with China and Russia; starts to think about closing borders and opening detention camps—white supremacy naturally comes fully back out into the open. That's the default mode—always—for a country built on genocide, slavery, annexation, colonialism, and every form of parasitism on people of color. If inter-imperialist rivalry is to be the order of the day, the US ruling class will need the militant loyalty of racist white people. Without that, the imperial center will not hold; the US will be unable to wage cold wars, trade wars, or physical wars against its hungry rivals.

And so, it's back to "normal" in amerika. We shouldn't waste our energy wishing it wasn't so. We should invest that energy in destroying any remaining illusions about a political system built from day one on oppressing non-white peoples and nations, here and all over the world. A system that must be uprooted, not reformed.

8. "NORMALIZING" OBAMA

And in the meantime, how about not "normalizing" Obama? Are the war crimes, assassinations, amnesty for torturers, mass incarceration, orwellian spy networks, out-of-control gangster cops, attacks on journalists and whistleblowers, and the vastly increased inequality that happened during his regime supposed to be some sort of baseline? Should we forget that he set a record for deportations? Are we going accept the bizarre narrative that Obama is really a well-meaning progressive "community organizer," who was frustrated and stymied by Republicans?

Notice that while we are girding ourselves to fight Trump, Obama is not. Do we see him boldly attacking Trump's racist, mysogynist plans, his reactionary appointments, his corruption, his militarism? Nope. He's making nice with The Donald. His attention has already turned to more important things, like his exciting plans for an opulent presidential library to praise his "legacy." Funded, of course, by the capitalists he has served so well.

We can project onto Obama that he's a tortured soul, wishing he could have done more to help people. But actually he's had a hugely successful career, and he's solidly loyal to monopoly capitalism. When multiculturalism served that cause, he was multiculturalism's very incarnation. Now, smart man that he is, he understands that his new job is to help manage a smooth transition from globalist multiculturalism to a system where open white supremacist nationalism can be mainstream again. And like a true professional, he's putting his personal feelings aside and taking care of business.

Much is made of the fact that, as he left office, Obama commuted a few thousand harsh sentences inflicted on people jailed for non-violent drug convictions. And gave out a handful of pardons. But even staying within the limits of bourgeois legality, he could have done so much more, if he cared.

A president's constitutional power to pardon people for federal offenses is practically unlimited. Pardon, not commute. When your sentence is commuted, you still have a criminal record. But when you are pardoned, your record is wiped clean. Even if you haven't been prosecuted yet, you can still be pardoned. One revealing example is Richard Nixon, pardoned cheerfully by Gerald Ford for "any crimes he may have committed against the United States while president." There are hundreds of thousands of victims of unjust, racist mass incarceration who could have been pardoned with a stroke of Obama's pen. Obama could have pardoned Leonard Peltier and all the other political prisoners; he could have pardoned Edward Snowden, too. There's nothing Trump could have done about it.

Why stop there? Millions of immigrants are directly threatened with deportation by the incoming regime. Trump has said he would start things off by deporting immigrant "criminals." Actually, the only "crime" committed by most undocumented immigrants is that they crossed the border illegally or overstayed their visa. Obama could have pardoned all those people, blocking their deportation. Nevertheless, when some Democratic congresspeople asked Obama to use his pardon power to protect a group of immigrants (in this case, the 750,000 young "Dreamers" who came to the US as children) he turned them down flat.

Obama isn't Trump's enemy, or his friend. He's simply an operative working for a fundamentally reactionary, white supremacist system. As popular resistance to Trump builds, we have to struggle to turn it into a deeper mass understanding of that system, instead of normalizing Obama or his sponsors. And we must find and unite with those who, based on that deeper understanding, are moving toward revolution; towards actually overthrowing white supremacy and capitalism entirely.

KEEP FASCISM DEAD

A Note on Sources

Throughout this book, sources referenced as "online" are provided without URLs. This is both to avoid clutter in the page layout, and because hyperlinks can change as web content is moved or removed.

Please also note that all sources recommended in the Glossary & Research Guide are similarly available online.

Interested readers can use a search engine with the article's title to find referenced material. If that doesn't work, the publisher maintains a complete list of sources cited.

Glossary & Research Guide

#Gamergate: An online campaign of harassment initiated in 2014, targeting women who worked in or were critical of sexism in the video game industry, coordinated partly with the #Gamergate Twitter hashtag. Supporters of Gamergate claimed that their campaign was a defense of free speech and journalistic ethics and against political correctness, but it included streams of misogynistic abuse, rape and death threats, as well as doxxing (public releases of personal information), which caused several women to leave their homes out of fear for their physical safety.

> READ MORE: Matt Lees, "What Gamergate should have taught us about the 'alt-right.'" *The Guardian*, December 1, 2016; http://www.wehuntedthemammoth.com/?s=gamergate

AlternativeRight.com: Website founded by Richard Spencer in 2010, along with Peter Brimelow and Paul Gottfried. Instrumental in the development of the "Alternative Right" current, the site quickly became a popular forum among dissident rightist intellectuals, especially younger ones. In 2012 Spencer turned *AlternativeRight.com* over to other editors, then shut it down completely, establishing a new online magazine, *Radix*.

> READ MORE: Devin Burghart, "Who is Richard Spencer?" *Institute For Research & Education On Human Rights*, June 27, 2014.

Alt-Lite: Conservatives and right-wingers who have acted as apologists for, or have helped to promote, the alt-right without embracing its full ideology or political programme. Alt-rightists have relied on the alt-lite to help bring their ideas to a mass, mainstream audience, but to varying degrees they have also regarded alt-lite figures with resentment, as ideologically untrustworthy opportunists.

READ MORE: Antifascist Front, "Introducing the Alt Lite, the People Mainstreaming the Alt Right's White Nationalism." *Anti-Fascist News*, November 3, 2016

American Renaissance: Founded by Jared Taylor, a so-called "race realist" (i.e. white nationalist) propaganda and intellectual organ, promoting pseudo-scientific studies and research that purport to show the inferiority of blacks to whites. *American Renaissance* was published as a monthly print magazine from October 1990 through January 2012; starting in 1994 it was also a website. American Renaissance has hosted periodic conferences, biennially from 1994–2008, and annually from 2012–2016. Attendees have included the likes of Richard Spencer, Paul Gottfried, Nick Griffin (British National Party), Bruno Gollnisch (France's *Front National*), Richard Lynn (editor of the *Mankind Quarterly*, journal of the Pioneer Fund), J. Philippe Rushton (Pioneer Fund), David Duke, and Don Black (KKK, *Stormfront* website), amongst many others. Today considered a part of the alt-right.

READ MORE: Antifascist Front, "Fascist Chic: Inside American Renaissance 2016." *Anti-Fascist News*, June 7, 2016; Antifascist Front, "American Renaissance's Jared Taylor Goes Full Anti-Semite." *Anti-Fascist News*, August 26, 2016; Antifascist Front, "Well Dressed Racism: American Renaissance Returns To Tennessee." *Anti-Fascist News*, January 31, 2016

American Vanguard: Formerly known as American Reaction, American Vanguard has close ties to *The Right Stuff* radio and podcast network (AV deputy director Cooper Ward is a co-host on *The Daily Shoah*) along with other white nationalist and neonazi formations. According to their website they meet regularly, have several chapters across the US, and have close connections to Counter-Currents Publishing, Identity Evropa, and other such groups. One of the alt-right groups to try to establish a presence off of the internet, following the 2016 Trump election, AV posters were found at Purdue University in Indiana, the University of Central Florida, Florida Gulf Coast University, the University of Arkansas at Fort Smith and Emerson College in Massachusetts.

> READ MORE: "University of Nebraska-Omaha Student Cooper Ward, Deputy Director Of American Vanguard." *It's Gong Down*, December 16, 2016; "The Loose Lips at American Vanguard Show Us Just How Fractured the Alt-Right Really Is." *It's Going Down*, December 28, 2016

Attack the System: Website of the American Revolutionary Vanguard, a project founded by "anarcho-pluralist" Keith Preston in the 1990s. ATS brings together a number of far right currents, ranging from National-Anarchists to libertarians, white nationalists to Duginists, and has long had a supportive relationship with the alt-right, however its own ideology is distinct from all of these, calling for a broad revolutionary alliance of all those who want to destroy US imperialism and the federal government. Within US borders, this would involve a "pan-secessionist" strategy uniting groups across the political spectrum who want to carve out self-governing enclaves free of US federal government control.

> READ MORE: Matthew N. Lyons, "Rising Above the Herd: Keith Preston's Authoritarian Anti-Statism." *New Politics*, April 29, 2011

Breitbart News: From its founding in 2007, *Breitbart* has featured sensationalist attacks on anyone to its left, praise for the Tea Party's anti-big government populism, and aggressive denials that conservatives are racist, sexist, or homophobic. Under Steve Bannon, who became executive chair in 2012, *Breitbart* began to scapegoat Muslims and immigrants more directly. In March 2016, *Breitbart* published "An Establishment Conservative's Guide to the Alt-Right," which helped boost the alt-right's profile and broaden its acceptability. Meanwhile, Steve Bannon declared *Breitbart* "the platform of the alt-right" and began publishing semi-veiled antisemitic attacks on Trump's opponents, all while insisting that white nationalists, antisemites, and homophobes were marginal to the alt-right. Despite this, *Breitbart News* as of this time is not considered by most alt-rightists as being more than a useful ally, rather than a full-fledged participant in their movement; it is part of the alt-lite.

READ MORE: http://www.breitbartunmasked.com/; Antifascist Front, "Breitbart Goes Full Fash." *Anti-Fascist News* April 5, 2016

Christian Reconstructionist: A far right pole within the US Christian Right, Reconstructionist ideology is an offshoot of Presbyterianism that was founded by Rev. R. J. Rushdoony in the 1960s. One of Reconstructionism's core principles is that Christianity is the basis for all knowledge and anything that departs from it is sinful, evil, satanic. Reconstructionists advocate a totalitarian theocracy based on their interpretation of the Bible: In their vision, only men from approved Christian churches could vote or hold office, slavery would once again be legal, and death (preferably by stoning) would be applicable punishment for homosexuality, adultery (by women), striking a parent, heresy, blasphemy, and many other offenses.

READ MORE: "Christian Reconstruction." Special Issue *The Public Eye* Vol. 8, No. 1: March/June 1994; Michael J. McVicar "The Libertarian Theocrats: The Long, Strange History of R.J. Rushdoony and Christian Reconstructionism." *Political Resarch Associates*, September 1, 2007

Counter-Currents Publishing: Founded by Greg Johnson (former editor of *The Occidental Quarterly*) in 2010 to "create an intellectual movement in North America that is analogous to the European New Right" and "lay the intellectual groundwork for a white ethnostate in North America." Part of the alt-right.

The Daily Stormer: Neonazi and white supremacist website founded in 2013, part of the alt-right; its name is a play on the German Nazi antisemitic newspaper *Der Sturmer*. *The Daily Stormer*'s editor and founder is Andrew Anglin (his previous less successful website was called "Total Fascism"). *The Daily Stormer* adopts a highly provocative tone, targeting a younger audience whose main area of political activity may be the internet. Anglin's calls via *The Daily Stormer* to harass specific individuals in the manner of #Gamergate have led to claims that he heads a "Troll Army." Most recently, this was on display in the harassment of Jews living in the Montana town of Whitefish (home of Richard Spencer's mother).

> READ MORE: Matt Pearce, "What happens when a millennial goes fascist? He starts up a neo-Nazi site." *Los Angeles Times*, June 24, 2015; Matthew Rozsa, "White nationalist wants to unleash his troll army on Jews in Montana." *Salon* Dec. 19, 2016

European New Right: The ENR began in France in 1968, with the intent to rehabilitate fascism and racism and make them appealing to future generations. Similar to the alt-right, the ENR is a far-flung constellation of groups, publications, and writers—"a school of thought, not an organization"—however, it is fair to say that its chief intellectual has been Alain de Benoist, its flagship publication *Nouvelle Ecole*, and its center of gravity the *Groupement de Recherche et Etudes sur la Civilization Européene* (GRECE; trans.: Research and Study Group on European Civilization). With a focus strictly on the alleged "elite", ENR adopted a metapolitical strategy; eclecticism and a "big tent" approach were firmly encouraged, as were overtures to non-fascist, and even left-wing, intellectuals and political traditions. Nonetheless, a core of positions held by most ENR members developed, these being sociobiology (pseudo-scientific racism), anti-Americanism, anti-capitalism, and anti-Christianity, all firmly grounded in an anti-egalitarian framework and resting on various theories about a distinct ancient "Indo-European" civilization. Over the years, the ENR came to constitute one of the most important political influences on the far right internationally.

READ MORE: Margaret Quigley, "Some Notes On The European 'New Right.'" *Political Research Associates*, January 1, 1991

Identitarian: A term that originated in France, where it was popularized by the far right *Bloc Identitaire* (founded in 2003); a subset of racist ideology focussing on specific national, as opposed to simply "white", identities, sometimes referring to ethnic communities that have not had their own states in modern times. While this has always been a tendency within the far right, in its current iteration Identitarianism draws on ideas popularized by the European New Right, and Identitarian organizations have worked alongside third positionist ones.

Identity Evropa: Founded in early 2016 by Nathan Damigo, an Iraqi war veteran based in California who had previously done time for violently attacking a Muslim man on the street. Closely connected to the American Freedom Party, so far, the main activity of Identity Evropa has been putting up posters on various college campuses, part of what it calls "Project Siege." Part of the alt-right; in May 2016, Damigo and Richard Spencer held a "free speech" event at the University of California, Berkeley, where the two, joined by supporters from the Traditionalist Youth Movement and Red Ice Radio, set up what they called a "safe space," purportedly to debate issues around race and white identity. As *It's Going Down* have noted, "Identity Evropa caters towards a very middle-class, (as in Abercrombie store manager,

not truck driver) if not upper middle-class audience. The group
has strict membership rules, such as no visible hand and neck
tattoos. This is important because the 'niche market' they are
attempting to reach is exclusively young, 'professional' men of
college age (and who are enrolled in higher education) that are
unhappy with 8 years of Obama and excited about the Trump
campaign."

READ MORE: "Identity Evropa: Mapping the Alt-Right Cadre."
Northern California Anti-Racist Action (NoCARA) Dec. 9, 2016

Libertarian: Unlike most of the world, in the United States, the
term libertarianism generally refers to right-wing philosophies,
rooted in classical liberalism, that call for an end to state inter-
ference with capitalism and property rights. Some libertarians
("minarchists") want to reduce the state to a few specific functions—mainly police, courts, and military—to safeguard persons
and property against aggression, while others ("anarcho-capital-
ists") want to abolish the state altogether. In addition to denying
non-state-based forms of oppression, libertarians generally reject
egalitarianism in principle. This orientation has helped make
libertarian ideas appealing to many far rightists, most notably
the Patriot movement and Christian Reconstructionists.

READ MORE: Jean Hardisty, "Libertarianism and Civil Society."
Public Eye, Vol. xII No. 1, Spring 1998

male tribalism: An anti-modern patriarchal philosophy associated with Jack Donovan, celebrating "the way of the gang," the
possibilities of failed states, and "anarcho-fascism." Donovan's
work has been embraced by the anti-state far rightists of *Attack
the System,* and he himself cites ENR theorist Guillaume Faye as
an influence on his vision of an ideal society, "The Brotherhood."

READ MORE: Matthew N. Lyons, "Jack Donovan on men:
a masculine tribalism for the far right." *Three Way Fight,*
November 23, 2015

Manosphere: A loose and informal network of blogs, web forums and websites, relating to issues of men and masculinity, within an anti-feminist framework, often rife with explicit and unrepentant misogyny. The manosphere includes various overlapping circles, such as Men's Rights Activists (MRAs), who argue that the legal system and media unfairly discriminate against men; Pickup Artists (PUAs), who help men learn how to manipulate women into having sex with them; Men Going Their Own Way (MGTOWs), who protest women's supposed dominance by avoiding relationships with them; and others.

READ MORE: "WTF is a MGTOW? A Glossary." *We Hunted the Mammoth*

Men's Rights Activists: MRA's argue that the legal system and media unfairly discriminate against men, within a framework ranging from simple anti-feminism to a broader view that this is part of a conspiracy against or degeneration of Western society.

READ MORE: Southern Poverty Law Center, "Leader's Suicide Brings Attention to Men's Rights Movement." *Intelligence Report*, Spring March 1, 2012

Metapolitics: A metapolitical approach involves a focus on ideas ranging from the "pre-political" to the cultural and philosophical, beliefs that often have nothing to do with elections or legislation, but which nonetheless undergird all formal politics. A metapolitical strategy is traditionally a matter of playing the long game, the goal being to shift the entire discussion in one's favour; however with the advent of social media and "meme magic," short-term metapolitical strategies can no longer be entirely ruled out. While the term "metapolitics" as it is used here owes its meaning largely to the European New Right, in and of itself there is nothing essentially right-wing about this strategy—in fact, it was partly informed by the ENR's appreciation for the ideas of Italian Communist Antonio Gramsci, from a far right perspective.

National-Anarchism: An offshoot of British neonazism that envisions a decentralized system of racially segregated communities. National-Anarchism established a small presence in the United States starting in 2007.

> READ MORE: Graham D. Macklin, "Co-opting the Counter Culture: Troy Southgate and the National Revolutionary Faction." *Patterns of Prejudice*, Vol.39, No.3, September 2005; Spencer Sunshine, "Rebranding Fascism: National-Anarchists." *Political Research Associates*, January 28, 2008

National Policy Institute: The white supremacist think-tank at the center of the alt-right. The NPI was founded in 2005 by William Regnery II; Louis R. Andrews was the chairman until 2010. When Andrews died in 2011, he was replaced by Richard Spencer. Following the 2016 Trump election, the NPI made international headlines when a video that was taken at their victory celebration in Washington DC showed Spencer shouting to a crowd of about 200 people: "Hail Trump, hail our people, hail victory!" as some attendees lifted their hands in a Nazi salute.

> READ MORE: Devin Burghart, "Who is Richard Spencer?" *Institute For Research & Education On Human Rights*, June 27, 2014; Jacob Siegel "The Alt-Right's Jewish Godfather," *Tablet*, Nov. 29, 2016; Josh Harkinson, "Meet the White Nationalist Trying to Ride the Trump Train to Lasting Power." *Mother Jones*, Oct. 27, 2016

Neo-Confederate: A branch of white nationalism that glorifies the Confederate States of America and, in some versions, advocates a new secession by southern states. Strongly nativist and conservative, neo-Confederates frame their politics in terms of defending their Southern white Christian traditions and identity.

> READ MORE: Max Blumenthal, "Neo-Confederates' existential crisis: Why they can't hide their racism any longer." *Salon*, July 9, 2015; Southern Poverty Law Center, "The Neo-Confederates." *Intelligence Report*, September 15, 2000 (Summer)

Neoreaction: Often abbreviated as NRx, and also known as Dark Enlightenment, neoreaction is a loosely unified school of thought that rejects egalitarianism in principle, argues that differences in human intelligence and ability are mainly genetic, and believes that cultural and political elites (which they call "the Cathedral") wrongfully limit the range of acceptable discourse. Blogger Curtis Yarvin (writing under the pseudonym Mencius Moldbug) launched neoreaction in 2007, but many other writers have contributed to it. Neoreaction emphasizes order and restoring the social stability that supposedly prevailed before the French Revolution, along with technocratic and futurist concerns such as transhumanism. NRx theorist Nick Land is a leading advocate of accelerationism, which in his version sees global capitalism driving ever-faster technological change, to the point that artificial intelligence replaces human beings.

READ MORE: Park MacDougald, "The Darkness Before the Right." *The Awl*, September 28, 2015

Occidental Dissent: Neo-Confederate and white nationalist blog run by Brad Griffin under the pseudonym Hunter Wallace.

The Occidental Quarterly: Published by the Charles Martel Society, *The Occidental Quarterly* is a leading organ of academic white nationalism and was influential in helping to develop the alt-right's intellectual wing. The current editor is Kevin MacDonald, a retired evolutionary psychologist and a prominent antisemite.

Paleoconservative: Although the term was coined by Paul Gottfried in 1986, paleoconservatives trace their lineage back to the "Old Right" of the 1930s, which opposed New Deal liberalism, and to the America First movement of the early 1940s, which opposed US entry into World War II. The term was adopted by Gottfried as a reaction against neoconservatives, those often formerly liberal and leftist intellectuals who were

gaining influential positions in right-wing think-tanks and in the
Reagan administration at the time. Paleoconservatism crested
with Pat Buchanan's presidential candidacy in 1992; in the post-
Soviet era they criticized military interventionism, free trade,
immigration, globalization, and the welfare state. They also
spoke out against Washington's close alliance with Israel, often
in terms that had anti-Jewish undertones. Paleoconservatives
tended to be unapologetic champions of European Christian
culture, and some of them gravitated toward white nationalism,
advocating a society in which white people, their values, interests,
and concerns would always be explicitly preeminent.

READ MORE: Dylan Matthews, "Paleoconservatism, the movement
that explains Donald Trump, explained." *Vox* May 6, 2016; Jacob
Siegel, "The Alt-Right's Jewish Godfather." *Tablet*, November 29,
2016

Patriot movement: Two years after a meeting of 160 "Christian
men" in Estes Park, Colorado—leaders from a broad range of far
right antigovernment groups—the Patriot movement appeared
as a national force in 1994, as activists began forming hundreds
of armed "militias" to defend against an expected crackdown,
or organized so-called common law courts that claimed legal
authority in place of the existing court system. The movement's
size and strength has waxed and waned, reaching a peak in the
mid-1990s, dropping almost to nothing in the early 2000s, and
surging to even higher levels during the Obama presidency.
The Patriot movement warns that there is a conspiracy by
globalist elites to disarm the American people, overthrow the
Constitution, and impose a dictatorship. It is a political hybrid,
a meeting place for several different rightist currents, including
activists from the antiabortion, wise use, libertarian, sovereign
citizen, and neonazi movements, amongst others.

READ MORE: Spencer Sunshine et al., "Up in Arms: A Guide to Oregon's Patriot Movement." *Political Research Associates/Rural Organizing Project* 2016; Spencer Sunshine, "Will the History Books Record How Neo-Nazis Made Eyes at the Bundy Militia?" *Truthout*, January 27, 2016; Matthew N. Lyons, "Oath Keepers, Ferguson, and the Patriot movement's conflicted race politics." *Three Way Fight*, August 28, 2015

Portland Students for Trump: Led by Matt Duffy and Volodymyr Kolychev at Portland State University, Portland Students for Trump has effectively used their small numbers to disrupt events organized by Black Lives Matter, and to stage their own stunts, like building a replica "Great Wall of Trump." Steeped in irreverent internet culture, the group promotes white supremacist arguments based on pseudo-science.

READ MORE: Arun Gupta, "Meet the shock troops of Trump's America." *The Raw Story*, June 17, 2016; Shane Burley and Alexander Reid Ross, "How the Alt Right is trying to create a 'safe space' for racism on college campuses." *Waging Nonviolence*, October 6, 2016

Proud Boys Network: Based around Gavin McInnes (founder and former editor of *Vice* magazine, and regular contributor to *Taki's Magazine*) and his internet television podcast, PBN is a club for men who oppose "political correctness," feminism, and anti-racism (these last two being taken to be anti-male and anti-white). Existing somewhere between the alt-lite and alt-right, PBN is a possible candidate for such politics taking material form outside of the internet.

READ MORE: Nicole Disser, "Gavin McInnes and His 'Proud Boys' Want to Make Men Great Again." *Bedford + Bowery*, July 28, 2016

PUA: Pickup Artists, who help men learn how to manipulate women into having sex with them, within an ideological framework ranging from simple anti-feminism to more elaborate directions. Best known for high-profile PUA author Roosh V (Daryush Valizadeh), who runs the website *Return of Kings*, and who has been described even by some in the alt-right as a rape advocate.

READ MORE: "The Gender Fascists of the Dark Enlightenment."
It's Going Down, February 4, 2016

Radix: Founded by Richard Spencer in 2012 as the alt-right propaganda arm of the National Policy Institute via Washington Summit Publishers, *Radix* exists today as an online magazine, a biannual print journal, and a publishing imprint, all devoted to promoting white supremacy and "radical traditionalism."

Red Ice: Founded by Henrik Palmgren in 2003, currently one of the largest podcast networks within the alt-right, with a strong European Identitarian emphasis. (The project is partly based in Sweden.) Currently its two main shows are Red Ice Radio (hosted by Henrik) and Radio 3Fourteen hosted by his wife Lana Lokteff. Guests have included Richard Spencer, American Renaissance's Jared Taylor, David Duke, Mike "Enoch" Peinovich and Jesse "Seventh Son" Dunstan from *The Daily Shoah*, Greg Johnson of *Counter-Currents*, various denizens of the manosphere, anti-vaccine activists, pagans, and Indo-Europeanists.

READ MORE: Antifascist Front, "Red Ice Creations And The New Fascist Media." *Anti-Fascist News*, July 11, 2016

Return of Kings: A leading manosphere website run by PUA author Roosh V (Daryush Valizadeh).

Stormfront: Neonazi discussion forum that was founded by former KKK leader Don Black in the early 1990s as an online bulletin board and became a website in 1996. *Stormfront* remains one of the largest white nationalist websites but has not become identified with the alt-right.

The Right Stuff: Alt-right blog and podcast, founded in 2013 by Mike "Enoch" Peinovich. Other co-hosts have included Cooper "Ghoul" Ward (of American Vanguard), Van "Bulbasaur" Bryant II, and Jesse "Seventh Son" Dunstan. TRS excels at being as offensive as possible. and "choose[s] to openly use racial slurs, degrade women and rape survivors, mock the holocaust and call for violence against Jews. Their podcast, *The Daily Shoah*, which is a play on *The Daily Show* and the Yiddish term for The Holocaust, is a roundtable discussion of different racists broadcasting under pseudonyms."

> READ MORE: Antifascist Front, "#Cuckservative: How the 'Alt Right' Took Off Their Masks and Revealed Their White Hoods." *Anti-Fascist News*, August 16, 2015; Slackbastard, "Mike Peinovich Unmasked As Leader Of 'The Right Stuff." *It's Gong Down*, January 14, 2017

Taki's Magazine: Founded in 2007, *Taki's Magazine* ("Takimag" for short) is an online magazine of politics and culture published by the Greek paleoconservative Taki Theodoracopulos and edited by Mandolyna Theodoracopulos, his daughter. The intent of the site, in Theodoracopulos's words, was to "shake up the stodgy world of so-called 'conservative' opinion…" "Takimag is a Libertarian webzine. We believe the best stories are smart, cheeky, and culturally relevant. We take our politics like we take life—lightly." The website garnered some controversy in 2013 after it published articles in support of the Greek ultranationalist political party Golden Dawn. From 2008 to 2010 its managing editor was Richard Spencer; amongst others, frequent contributors include Gavin McInnes (Proud Boys Network), Jim Goad (author of *The Redneck Manifesto*), Kathy Shaidle (the Canadian blogger behind the racist fivefeetoffury.com), John Derbyshire (formerly of the *National Review*), and Steve Sailer (columnist for VDARE.com, and founder of the pseudo-scientific racist Human Biodiversity Institute).

Third Position: Rejecting both communism and capitalism, Italian and British fascists initiated Third Position politics in the 1970s, and Tom Metzger's White Aryan Resistance subsequently brought it to prominence within the US far right in the 1980s. That said, Third Position claims to trace its lineage all the way back to the German Nazi movement's "left" wing, which was associated with the brothers Gregor and Otto Strasser in the early 1930s, and which emphasized class struggle against conservative elites and capitalists. While retaining a virulently antisemitic and racist worldview, Third Position also refers positively to Peronism, the Arab anticolonial movement, and Mao, amongst others.

READ MORE: Chip Berlet, "What Is The Third Position?" *Political Research Associates*, December 19, 2016

Traditionalist Youth Network: Established in 2013 by Matthew Heimbach and Matt Parrott, the TYN draws heavily on third positionism and Identitarianism. Although initially associated with the American Freedom Party, in 2015 the TYN established the Traditionalist Workers Party (TWP) as its own political-party offshoot. TYN/TWP advocates unity between white supremacist forces including neonazis, though tries to frame its own politics in terms of white Christian traditionalism. One of the few groups within the alt-right to attempt to exist in the real world outside of the internet; in June 2016 an attempted TWP "protest against globalization and in defense of the right to free expression" in Sacramento turned into an attack on antifascist counterprotesters, several of whom were stabbed.

READ MORE: "The New Neo-Nazis: How Matthew Heimbach Is Building a Racist Network Across the US." *It's Going Down*, September 13, 2015; Shane Burley and Alexander Reid Ross, "How the Alt Right is trying to create a 'safe space' for racism on college campuses." *Waging Nonviolence*, October 6, 2016

VDARE: A foundation and website run by Peter Brimelow, inspired in part by his 1995 book *Alien Nation*, and devoted to opposing non-white immigration and promoting white supremacist politics. Contributors to the website have included Steve Sailer, Jared Taylor (American Renaissance), J. Philippe Rushton (Pioneer Fund), Kevin MacDonald, Samuel T. Francis (Council of Conservative Citizens), and many others.

A Voice for Men: Website founded in 2009 by Men's Rights Activist Paul Elam, and a major forum of the manosphere.

Vox Popoli: The blog of Theodore Robert Beale (aka "Vox Day"), a science fiction author active in the alt-right. Day has gained some notoriety for attempts to run slates of far right authors (many of whom are associated with his Castalia House publishing company) for the annual science fiction Hugo Awards.

Washington Summit Publishers: Publishing arm of the National Policy Institute.

> READ MORE: Devin Burghart, "Who is Richard Spencer?" *Institute For Research & Education On Human Rights*, June 27, 2014

Wermod and Wermod: Small publishing house run by Alex Kurtagic, specializing in racist material. While there are some contemporary writers (Joseph Bowden, Troy Southgate, Kurtagic himself), most titles are historical "classics" (Francis Parker Yockey, H.S. Chamberlain, H.P. Lovecraft).

> READ MORE: Devin Burghart, "Who is Richard Spencer?" *Institute For Research & Education On Human Rights*, June 27, 2014

White Nationalism: A form of white supremacist ideology that advocates a concept of nationhood based on membership in the supposed white race. White nationalists claim that European culture and white people's strengths and virtues are the basis for all that is great about the United States. Some white nationalists want to restore white people's explicit dominance and primacy within the framework of the existing US political system. Other white nationalists want to overthrow the established political order and either replace it with a new all-white nation or break it up into multiple racially defined "ethnostates."

White Supremacy: Both a *social system* and an *ideology*. The *system* of white supremacy, also known as white racial oppression, gives people defined as "white" a status of relative privilege over all other people, and was created in the early capitalist era to help bolster the power of economic and political elites. A white supremacist system may be explicit or implicit. The specific privileges associated with whiteness may be legal, economic, cultural, and/or social, and may vary widely depending on the specific historical context. The *ideology* of white supremacy explicitly states that racial categories are inherent, primary determinants of human experience rather than social constructs; that white people are superior to and more important than people of color; and that whites should either hold formal power and privilege over people of color or should eliminate them entirely. As a system, white supremacy is and always has been central to the US social order, but white supremacist ideology is no longer dominant. A majority of white people embrace other ideologies, such as colorblindness and multiculturalism, which help to support subtler and more sophisticated forms of white supremacy as a system.

Wolves of Vinland: Odinist and white nationalist group based in Virginia, whose members include Jack Donovan and whose internal culture—centered on ritualistic, violent male bonding— matches many aspects of Donovan's male tribalist ideal.

READ MORE: "The Wolves of Vinland: A Fascist Countercultural 'Tribe' in the Pacific Northwest." Rose City Antifa, November 7, 2016

FURTHER READING

Anti-Fascist Forum, *My Enemy's Enemy: Essays on Globalization, Fascism and the Struggle Against Capitalism*

Chip Berlet ed. *Eyes Right! Challenging the Right Wing Backlash*

Chip Berlet and Matthew N. Lyons, *Right-Wing Populism in America: Too Close for Comfort*

Sara Diamond, *Roads to Dominion: Right-Wing Movements and Political Power in the United States*

Martin Durham, *White Rage: The Extreme Right and American Politics*

Abby L. Ferber, *Home-Grown Hate: Gender and Organized Racism*

Roger Griffin, *The Nature of Fascism*

Don Hamerquist, J. Sakai, Xtn, and Mark Salotte, *Confronting Fascism: Discussion Documents for a Militant Movement*

Michael Novick *White Lies, White Power: The Fight Against White Supremacy and Reactionary Violence*

James Ridgeway. *Blood in the Face: The Ku Klux Klan, Aryan Nations, Nazi Skinheads and the Rise of a New White Culture*

Alexander Reid Ross, *Against the Fascist Creep*

M. Testa, *Militant Anti-Fascism: A Hundred Years of Resistance*

Leonard Zeskind, *Blood and Politics: The History of the White Nationalist Movement from the Margins to the Mainstream*

ANTIFASCIST RESOURCES

The editors began assembling a list of organizations doing antifascist work and research in the United States, however soon the number of groups became far too long to include here. What follows is therefore an incomplete list; a more extensive list is being maintained at:

THREEWAYFIGHT.BLOGSPOT.COM/P/ANTIFASCIST-RESOURCES_20.HTML

Angry White Men
(((Tracking the Alt Right)))
https://angrywhitemen.org

Anti-Fascist News
https://antifascistnews.net

Anti-Racist Action Los Angeles /
People Against Racist Terror
P.O. Box 1055
Culver City, CA 90232

www.antiracist.org

International Anti-Fascist
Defence Fund
intlantifadefence.wordpress.com

It's Going Down
https://itsgoingdown.org/

NYC Antifa
https://nycantifa.wordpress.com

One People Project
P.O. Box 42817
Philadelphia, PA 19101

www.onepeoplesproject.com

Philly Antifa
https://phillyantifa.noblogs.org

Political Research Associates
1310 Broadway, Suite 201
Somerville, MA 02144

www.politicalresearch.org

Rose City Antifa
www.rosecityantifa.org

Three Way Fight
www.threewayfight.blogspot.com

Torch Antifascist Network
www.torchantifa.org

Twin Cities
General Defense Committee
https://twincitiesgdc.org/
https://www.facebook.com/TC.GDC
https://twitter.com/tcgdc

We Hunted the Mammoth
tracking the "manosphere"
www.wehuntedthemammoth.com

GLOBAL ANTIFA PRISONER LIST, AND INFORMATION ABOUT THE ANNUAL JULY 25TH INTERNATIONAL DAY OF SOLIDARITY WITH ANTIFASCIST PRISONERS
HTTPS://NYCANTIFA.WORDPRESS.COM/GLOBAL-ANTIFA-PRISONER-LIST

INDEX

INSURGENT SUPREMACISTS:
The U.S. Far Right's Challenge to State and Empire

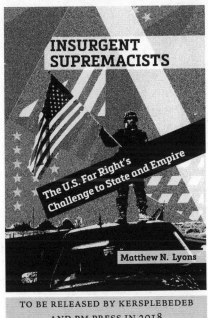

INSURGENT SUPREMACISTS

The U.S. Far Right's Challenge to State and Empire

Matthew N. Lyons

TO BE RELEASED BY KERSPLEBEDEB
AND PM PRESS IN 2018

A major study of movements that strive to overthrow the U.S. government, that often claim to be anti-imperialist and sometimes even anti-capitalist ... and which also consciously promote inequality, hierarchy, and domination, generally along explicitly racist, sexist, and homophobic lines. Revolutionaries of the far right: insurgent supremacists.

In this book, Matthew N. Lyons takes readers on a tour of neonazis and Christian theocrats, by way of the Patriot Movement, the Larouchites, and the Alt-Right. Supplementing this, thematic sections expore specific dimensions of far right politics, regarding gender, decentralism, and anti-imperialism.

Finally, intervening directly in debates within left and antifascist movements, Lyons examines both the widespread use and abuse of the term "fascism," and the relationship between federal security forces and the paramilitary right.

Both for its analysis and as a guide to our opponents, *Insurgent Supremacists* promises to be a powerful tool in organizing to resist the forces at the cutting edge of reaction today.

**KER
SPL
EBE
DEB**

Since 1998 Kersplebedeb has been an important source of radical literature and agit prop materials.

The project has a non-exclusive focus on anti-patriarchal and anti-imperialist politics, framed within an anticapitalist perspective. A special priority is given to writings regarding armed struggle in the metropole, and the continuing struggles of political prisoners and prisoners of war.

The Kersplebedeb website presents historical and contemporary writings by revolutionary thinkers from the anarchist and communist traditions.

Kersplebedeb can be contacted at:

Kersplebedeb
CP 63560
CCCP Van Horne
Montreal, Quebec
Canada
H3W 3H8

email: info@kersplebedeb.com
web: www.kersplebedeb.com
         www.leftwingbooks.net

Kersplebedeb